NARINDER SINGH CHOHAN

The Invisible Prison

How Ancient Wisdom Helped Me Break Free from OCD and Overthinking

First published by NSC Publishing 2026

This book is intended for informational and educational purposes only. It is not a substitute for professional medical, psychological, or psychiatric advice, diagnosis, or treatment.

The author shares personal experiences and insights, but every individual's situation is different. If you are experiencing severe anxiety, OCD, or any mental health condition, please seek guidance from a qualified healthcare professional.

The ideas presented in this book are meant to support personal understanding and awareness, not to replace professional care.

Some teachings and quotations in this book are drawn from early Buddhist texts, including the Dhammapada, the Pali Canon, and various suttas. These works are in the public domain and are included for educational and reflective purposes.

First edition

ISBN: 978-0-6451914-3-1

This book was professionally typeset on Reedsy.
Find out more at reedsy.com

To the seekers, the questioners, and those who suffer quietly. May the simple act of observing your mind begin to unravel the chains that bind you in the invisible prison.

Contents

III Understanding the Mind

IV The Path to Calm and Clarity

Preface

Why I Needed to Write This Book

I didn't write this book because I consider myself a teacher. I didn't write it because I think I'm spiritually advanced. I didn't write it because I have all the answers.

I wrote it because, at one point in my life, I desperately needed a book like this. A book that spoke honestly about the chaos inside the mind. A book that didn't pretend healing was simple, didn't use heavy spiritual language, and didn't promise miracles. A book that didn't judge me for struggling.

I wanted a book that shared a personal journey. A journey of suffering, confusion, hope, and ultimately, clarity. Something I could relate to, something that made me feel understood and reminded me I wasn't alone in the messiness of my own mind. A book that acknowledged the hard, confusing, and often lonely path of understanding yourself, while still offering a quiet sense of hope that freedom was possible.

I wish someone had told me, many years ago, that my suffering wasn't a sign of weakness or a lack of faith. I wish someone had explained that thoughts are not commands, that fear is not truth, and that guilt doesn't always mean punishment. I wish someone had told me that healing doesn't come from running toward new religions, new rules, or new identities. It comes from understanding yourself.

My journey has been long. I've moved through Sikhism,

Hindu traditions, Christianity in its many forms, Torah groups, and even small touches of Islam. Every path gave me something. And every path, in its own way, also left me with more questions.

But the deepest turning point didn't come from strict rules, rituals, identity, or the promise of heaven somewhere far away. It came from learning to observe my own mind.

I began to see that I am not my thoughts or emotions. I am the one who notices them, the quiet observer. Thoughts come and go like clouds, but something within me remains still. That is awareness, always present.

This understanding didn't come all at once. It began in a simple, unexpected way, by watching my wife. She has a natural way of observing life. Calm, attentive, never rushing, never judging. She doesn't dwell on the past or worry about the future; she stays present. She notices her thoughts and feelings without being consumed by them. She moves through life with a quiet clarity that I could only admire. Watching her, I started to see that there is a way to witness the mind without being trapped by it.

And it deepened through the words of a monk here in Melbourne, whose quiet teachings shook the foundation of my suffering. He pointed me back to a simple, ancient truth: suffering can be understood, and there is a way out of it.

The peace I spent years chasing outside was actually an inner skill. The skill of understanding the mind.

From the moment I was born, through childhood and into adulthood, people around me, parents, teachers, and religious leaders, taught me many things about life. They taught me what to do, what to believe, and what to avoid.

But no one taught me how to understand my own mind.

No one taught me how to notice my thoughts without getting lost in them. How to observe fear, guilt, and anxiety without letting them take control. This is why so many of us struggle. We repeat the same patterns, chase peace outside ourselves, and never realize that true peace has always been within us.

Peace isn't something we create. It's something we learn to recognize and practice. It has always been there, quietly present, waiting for us to notice.

I'm not here to convert you. I'm not here to tell you what to believe. I'm not here to prove which religion is true or false. I'm not here to start a new belief system. I'm not here to debate or challenge any religion or religious leader. I'm simply here to open a window, just enough for you to see that freedom is possible, even for minds like ours.

If my story helps even one person feel less alone, or gives someone a small breath of relief, or makes someone say, "**Okay... maybe there's hope for me too**," then writing this book is worth it.

Thank you for opening these pages. Thank you for trusting me with your time and your heart.

Let's walk out of this invisible prison together.

Acknowledgments

Writing this book has been a journey I could never have completed on my own.

First, I want to thank my wife. Your calm presence, unwavering patience, and quiet love guided me through the heaviest moments of my mind. You showed me that even in the darkest spaces, freedom and peace are possible.

I am deeply grateful to the monk in Melbourne, Australia, whose gentle wisdom and subtle teachings reshaped the way I understand myself, my mind, and my suffering. Your guidance illuminated paths I didn't know existed.

To my family and friends, thank you for listening without judgment, supporting me when I struggled, and believing in me even when I couldn't see the way forward. Your encouragement made this book possible.

And to you, the reader, thank you for opening these pages. Thank you for trusting me with your time and your heart. My hope is that within these words, you find a small measure of understanding, comfort, and clarity, a reminder that even in an invisible prison, freedom is possible.

Introduction

The Prison You Can't See

Most prisons have walls, doors, and guards. This one doesn't. There are no bars to rattle, no locks to pick, no visible signs that you're trapped at all. In fact, from the outside, life can look perfectly normal. You show up. You perform your roles. You do what is expected of you.

Yet inside, there is a constant sense of being confined, not by circumstances, but by your own thoughts.

This is the kind of prison that convinces you everything is your fault. That you are weak for feeling the way you do. That if you were just stronger, more faithful, more disciplined, or more positive, you would finally be free. And so you keep trying. You keep fixing. You keep searching. All while quietly believing that something is deeply wrong with you.

I didn't have words for this prison back then. I only knew how it felt to live inside it.

There are two kinds of suffering in this world. The first is the kind everyone can see, a broken leg, a financial crisis, a relationship ending. People notice it, they understand it, and they offer help. And then there is the second kind, the suffering that hides.

The kind that lives in your thoughts.

The kind that keeps you awake while everyone else is sleeping.

The kind that makes your chest feel tight even when nothing is happening.

The kind that makes you question your value, your sanity, your place in this world.

I lived with that hidden suffering for years. On the outside, I was functioning. Going to work, being a husband, being a father. Smiling when I needed to. Holding conversations as if everything was fine. People saw the "normal" version of me, the one who seemed calm and collected, never noticing the constant unrest inside. I kept up the routines, played my part, and tried to appear okay, even when every quiet moment reminded me that I wasn't.

But inside, I was wrestling with a mind that never stopped. Thoughts that came like waves. Fears that felt real even when I knew they weren't. Guilt that I carried without even understanding why. Every quiet moment felt invaded by doubt, as if my mind refused to give me rest. Memories I wished I could forget would surface uninvited, replaying mistakes and "what-ifs" over and over.

Even the simplest decisions felt heavy, weighed down by an invisible pressure I couldn't explain. It was like living in an invisible prison that no one else could see, a prison that shaped every feeling, every heartbeat, every breath, yet left no trace on the outside world.

I didn't know it then, but I was trapped in what I now call the invisible prison. For a long time, I tried to escape it through religions, rituals, new beliefs, and new systems, hoping each one would finally bring me peace and a sense of freedom I couldn't find on my own. I moved from one practice to another, following advice, reading teachings, repeating mantras, believing that maybe the next path would fix me.

I even tried to break free by fighting the prison itself, trying to control my thoughts, silence them, or suppress them. I did everything I could. But no matter what I tried, the relief was always temporary.

The mind, restless and heavy, would return, bringing the same fears, the same guilt, the same questions I thought I had left behind. I kept thinking, "**Maybe this will fix me. Maybe this path will finally give me peace.**" But each time, the peace was temporary, and the fear returned stronger.

For a long time, I believed freedom would come from changing who I was. From becoming a better version of myself. A calmer version. A more spiritual version. A version without these thoughts or fears.

What I slowly came to see was something very different.

The problem was never the thoughts themselves. It was my relationship with them. The constant struggle. The resistance. The belief that every thought needed to be answered, fixed, or controlled. Without realizing it, I was fighting my own mind every day and calling that fight survival.

Buddhist wisdom didn't give me a new identity or a new set of rules to follow, or a promise of becoming something beyond human. It gave me something far more valuable: clarity. A way to see thoughts as thoughts, not as commands. A way to sit with discomfort without drowning in it. A way not to reject suffering, but to understand it. A way to meet fear without becoming it. It showed me that my mind could be observed rather than controlled, and that the constant chatter and judgment I had lived with for years didn't define who I was.

It taught me patience, not the kind that waits for something to change, but the kind that allows me to be fully present with what is, without resistance or self-criticism. It gave me the tools to navigate uncertainty with compassion, to hold space for my own struggles while remaining grounded. In short, it offered freedom, the freedom to live in my own mind without being imprisoned by it, and the quiet assurance that I could face whatever arises with clarity, steadiness, and self-compassion.

That understanding didn't arrive all at once. It came quietly, gently, through observation, patience, and compassion, especially toward myself.

That is when I finally understood something important. I wasn't broken. My mind was simply overwhelmed. And freedom was never something I had to earn; it was something I needed to understand.

This book is not about proving any religion wrong. It's not about preaching a new belief system. It's a story about suffering, confusion, hope, and finally, clarity. It's about looking within, understanding the mind, and discovering that the answers you've been seeking are often closer than you think.

If you have ever felt trapped inside your own head, if you've ever questioned your worth, if you've lived with intrusive thoughts, fear, trauma, spiritual pressure, obsessive thinking, or endless rumination, this book is for you. It is for anyone who has felt alone in their struggles, anyone who has believed that no one could understand the silent battles within.

You are not alone. And most importantly, you are not stuck. There is a way out of the invisible prison. I found it in unexpected places, in quiet moments, in simple teachings, in experiences that seemed ordinary at first. And now, I want to share it with you, so that you too can begin to see your mind clearly, face your suffering with compassion, and move toward the freedom that has always been there.

Life will bring pain. That cannot be avoided. But how we live with it, how we see it, and how we allow it to shape us, is something we can learn.

The invisible prison is real. But so is the key.

And as you turn these pages, you will begin to find it for yourself.

I

My Personal Journey

This section sets the stage by sharing the problem through my own life. It shows how my mind was untrained, how my beliefs began to break, and how suffering became overwhelming. From early struggles to love, faith, doubt, and the guidance of a monk, it paints a picture of restlessness and inner conflict, leading us to explore the mind more deeply.

1

Unlocking the Invisible Prison

Most of us never realise how deeply we can suffer inside our own minds. On the outside, life seems fine. You go to work, look after your family, smile for photos, and do what everyone expects.

But inside, there can be a storm no one else can see. A storm of thoughts, fears, doubts, and memories that keep returning no matter how much you try to move on. The mind pulls you into the past with regrets and past mistakes that replay endlessly, and pushes you into the future with worries and "what-ifs" that won't let you rest. Self-criticism whispers in every quiet moment, making it all feel impossible to escape.

For years, I lived in that storm. I didn't understand it at first. I just knew something felt wrong. Looking back now, I can see that I was trapped in an invisible prison. Not a prison built by society, culture, religion, or any other person, circumstance, or bad choice. It was a prison slowly built by my own mind, made of intrusive thoughts that appeared out of nowhere, fears that felt so real they became my truth, guilt that never seemed to run out, and overthinking that drained every bit of peace.

It was built from a past that held on even when I tried to let it go, from endless mental loops and rumination circling in my mind, and from silent rituals and compulsions that never showed on the outside but dominated my inner life.

From the outside, no one would ever guess. I looked "fine," yet inside I was fighting battles that felt impossible to win.

This prison is cruel because it's silent. It has no walls you can touch, no rules you can break, and no guards to blame. It lives inside you, follows you everywhere, and whispers at the worst possible moments.

It has neither light nor darkness, no beginning or end, no doors to open, and no windows to look out of. It grows quietly, almost invisibly, feeding on your doubts, fears, and unspoken thoughts.

It bends time and memory, making minutes feel like hours and memories feel like the present. It drags you into the past or pushes you into the future, never allowing you to live fully in the present moment. It is everywhere yet nowhere, relentless yet unseen, a shadow clinging to your mind.

Even in the simplest tasks, washing dishes, driving, talking with someone, watching TV, eating at a restaurant with my family, or sitting quietly with a cup of coffee, the storm could appear. A memory, a fear, or a small worry could flood my mind, making me feel trapped even in ordinary moments. It could happen in the middle of laughter, on a walk in the park, or while scrolling through my phone. Calm, everyday moments would suddenly feel tense, consumed by anxiety. No place ever felt completely safe, because the storm existed inside me, separate from what was happening around me.

You can't walk away from it. You can't take a break from it. You can't pray it away or switch religions and expect it to disappear. You carry it with you every second.

The more you try to escape this prison, the stronger it becomes. This invisible prison is a master illusionist. It uses time, memory, fear, and old wounds to create stories and images that feel real. It tricks you into believing everything it shows you.

And for a long time, I believed it. I thought this was simply how life is, that something in my mind was permanently broken, that I was weaker than everyone else. I thought maybe God was disappointed in me, or that I was being punished for something I didn't understand.

But none of that was true. The invisible prison was never a punishment. It was simply misunderstood pain. Pain that had never been seen or understood, never met with kindness, and never held in awareness long enough for me to recognise what it was trying to tell me.

The day I finally began to look at that pain instead of running from it was the day the walls of my prison began to loosen. I started to sit with my pain instead of avoiding it. I allowed myself to remain inside the invisible prison instead of trying to escape it every second.

Because the moment you understand your prison, you've already taken the first step out of it. You don't truly understand your suffering until you find a way to rise above it.

Think of it like this: a tadpole lives its whole life in water, yet it doesn't know what "water" is until it grows legs, rises to the surface, and experiences the world outside. Only then does it realise what it had been surrounded by all along.

A newborn baby doesn't understand what a mother is or that an entire world exists beyond its tiny vision. It sees only blurry shapes and feels warmth. But as the baby grows, its senses open, and it realises there is far more than what it once knew.

A caterpillar crawls its whole life on leaves, believing small, slow movement is all it will ever experience. It has no idea that within its struggle, a completely different life is waiting, one with wings, freedom, and sky. Only when it breaks out of its cocoon does it finally understand what it was meant to become.

A person lost in dense fog can barely see a few steps ahead, and everything feels confusing and unsafe. But when the fog lifts, the path that once felt frightening becomes clear and gentle. The world didn't change. Their clarity did.

Just like the tadpole, the newborn baby, the caterpillar discovering its wings, and the traveller waiting for the fog to lift, I, too, had to rise above my suffering to finally understand it. Only then did I realise that the prison I feared most was built from my own misunderstanding.

It's like standing at the base of a giant mountain. From below, your view is limited. You can't see what lies beyond or around you. But as you climb higher, your perspective changes. At the peak, everything becomes clear.

Our suffering works the same way. When you're inside it, you can't see it clearly. But once you rise above it, even a little, you begin to understand what was holding you for so long.

This book is the story of how I found the key, not in religion, mental force, rituals, strict rules, chanting, or the promise of heaven. I didn't find it in self-help slogans, in forcing myself to think positively, in running away to new places, in burying myself in work or achievements, or in pretending to be strong while breaking inside. It didn't come from therapy worksheets, expensive retreats, motivational speeches, or waiting for someone else to save me.

The key was much simpler than all of that. It was learning to sit quietly and observe my mind, without identifying with every thought, reacting to every feeling, or trying to control or suppress whatever arose. It was simply noticing, allowing, and being present with what is, letting the mind reveal itself naturally.

Because your thoughts have the power to colour your entire world. You become tinted by the colours you repeatedly think in. If your thoughts are soaked in fear, the world looks frightening. If they're shaped by anger, everything feels like an attack. If they're filled with shame, you begin to hide from yourself. But when your thoughts become clear, your inner world becomes clear too. The colour shifts, and so does your reality.

It's like wearing tinted glasses. The world may be bright, but dark lenses make everything appear dim. Or like tea leaves dropped into water. The water becomes the colour of whatever enters it. Our minds are the same. Whatever thoughts we allow to settle within us shape our entire experience.

Learning to sit with my mind instead of fighting it, to watch my thoughts without becoming them, to notice the storm without being pulled into it, that was the beginning of freedom. The freedom I searched for was never out there. It wasn't in the things we chase, the promises we hope for, or the answers we expect from the world. It was inside me all along, quietly waiting to be discovered.

Even when I began to notice my thoughts instead of being swallowed by them, it wasn't an instant transformation. There were days when the storm still raged, when fear, guilt, and doubt tried to pull me back into old patterns. But now, I could see them for what they were, passing clouds in the sky of my mind, not permanent structures, not truths I had to obey. Each quiet observation became a small step out of the prison. Each moment of clarity became a crack in the walls that had once felt so solid.

And I realised I was not alone. Many of us carry this hidden storm, though few speak of it. Recognising it is the first step toward stepping out of it. Each moment of awareness, no matter how small, becomes a quiet victory, a signal that freedom is possible.

In the end, quiet observation became the greatest victory of the mind. The mind stays the same. It's our clarity that transforms. When you see the mind clearly, it stops being your enemy. It is both the builder and the destroyer. Clarity decides which role it plays.

And the most transformed person is the one who has tasted ruin, healed alone, and still chose to become whole again.

2

Born into Two Worlds

I was born and raised in a Hindu-Sikh family in Punjab, India, a world where religion, rituals, and cultural expectations were part of everyday life. From an early age, I learned that being "good" meant following rules, performing rituals correctly, and respecting the stories and teachings of our faith.

Spirituality wasn't presented as a personal choice, but as a framework I was expected to follow: worshipping gods, attending temples, reciting prayers, and understanding that failing in these duties could bring judgment, punishment, or negative consequences. I was also taught about heaven and hell, how good actions would lead to rewards in the afterlife, while mistakes or disobedience could bring suffering or punishment.

Fear of hell, punishment, and divine disapproval was subtly woven into our daily lives. Even as a child, I sensed that spiritual rules carried real consequences.

One memory that stays with me happened when I was around 13 or 14. My family was driving to a temple in the mountains, a sacred place devoted to a goddess. A car suddenly stopped us on the road. The driver approached and demanded a monetary offering. He said there was a woman in the car who had "seen" us and knew we were devout worshippers. If we didn't give her money, 500 rupees at the time, we would be cursed and might have an accident. My uncle, who was financially well-off, gave the money out of fear. The memory of that fear, and the anxiety it sparked in all of us, stayed with me for years.

I also remember how other family members strongly believed in superstitions. For example, if a cat crossed our path, we were told not to go ahead and to wait, or bad luck might follow. Similarly, if a broom fell to the floor, it was considered a bad omen, and we had to follow certain rituals to avoid trouble.

Sweeping the house after sunset was forbidden, as it was believed to sweep away wealth or invite bad luck. Seeing a black dog or an owl cross our path was considered a warning of danger. Even sneezing at the wrong moment, like before leaving the house, was interpreted as a sign of trouble ahead. Certain times on the clock were considered unlucky, and going out at those times was strongly avoided. Stepping over red cloth laid on the floor or ignoring small traditional precautions could also bring negative consequences.

These small but persistent beliefs shaped my early mind, teaching me that unseen forces could influence everyday life. They created a sense of caution, fear, and constant vigilance, making it feel as though the world was full of invisible rules that had to be carefully followed to stay safe.

Stories of curses, karmic retribution, and divine punishment were part of everyday conversation. Even casual misbehaviour or small mistakes could feel like a spiritual failure. For a young mind, this created a constant sense of anxiety, a quiet, unspoken pressure to be perfect, to obey, and to fear unseen consequences.

Another memory that shaped me happened during Diwali, the festival of lights. My family insisted that every lamp, every offering, and every prayer had to be done exactly right. I recall lighting the lamps incorrectly once and being told that a small mistake could bring trouble to the house. I felt a weight in my chest I didn't understand, an invisible chain of guilt that stayed with me long after the festival ended.

There were countless small moments like this. Lighting a lamp at the wrong time, spilling a bit of oil while offering it, placing meat next to food in the fridge that had been offered, or even arranging sweets in the "wrong" order were enough to cause worry and tension.

God, in my early years, felt both close and distant, an ever-watchful presence who measured my actions, rewarded obedience, and punished mistakes. I was taught to fear God's displeasure almost as much as I was taught to revere His blessings.

In that world, God was not only love and guidance but also judgment and consequence. Every small error, every forgotten ritual, every lapse in attention felt like a potential offence. And yet, in quiet moments, I glimpsed another side, a sense that God could also be mercy, presence, and comfort.

That tension, the fear of punishment, and the longing for connection, shaped the way I saw myself, my choices, and the world around me. It planted early questions about what it really means to know God, to be free, and to live without invisible chains.

Even as I grew older, these experiences were not just stories or childhood fears. They became the foundation of how I saw the world. Every act, every thought, seemed to carry a deeper consequence. And beneath it all, a quiet seed of fear had taken root, shaping how I related to myself and my choices.

Growing up, I felt like I was born into two worlds: one of love, family, and celebration, and another of rules, fear, and spiritual obligation. This constant tension shaped my mind, teaching me to live between love and fear, and planting the early questions I would later explore about freedom, suffering, and the mind.

All these rules, rituals, and constant efforts to avoid misfortune or gain favour didn't bring clarity. They brought more struggle. Each action, each precaution, each repeated prayer felt like a step toward some imagined "heaven," yet it was exhausting, never-ending, and often confusing.

The more I tried to follow everything perfectly, the more tension, doubt, and fear grew inside me. My mind became a battlefield of conflicting instructions, expectations, and inner judgments.

True observation, presence, and freedom, the very things I would later discover were possible, felt further away with every attempt to obey, control, or earn approval. I was chasing an external idea of perfection and reward, while real freedom was quietly slipping away, hidden beneath the weight of my own efforts.

3

The First Cracks in the Mind

The first cracks in my mind didn't appear suddenly. They didn't arrive with a dramatic event or a single moment of collapse. They showed up quietly, through small anxieties, restless thoughts, and a growing heaviness I couldn't name at the time. Looking back, this is when the invisible prison began building its first walls.

I was around seventeen when everything shifted. Until then, I was a brilliant student, one of the top in my school. My teachers believed I had a bright future ahead. Many of them imagined I would go into engineering or another respected profession. And truthfully, I believed that too. I had dreams, ambition, and a sense of direction. But life doesn't always follow the dreams of a young mind.

My family simply did not have the financial stability to support my education. At that time, and even now, colleges and universities were all in the city, far from our village. Living and studying there felt completely out of reach for ordinary middle-class families like ours.

We lived in a joint family with limited space, shared responsibilities, and constant pressure. My father was a government employee who did everything he could, but our circumstances were still difficult. When the time came to enrol in an engineering college, the truth was simple. We just could not afford it, even though it was what I truly wanted to study and the dream I was passionate about.

Instead of classrooms, textbooks, and the future I had prepared for, I found myself inside my uncle's jewellery workshop, learning to mould, file, shape, and polish gold. At an age when my friends were stepping into college life, I was stepping into a world of labour, long hours, and responsibilities I wasn't ready for.

My days became a routine of exhaustion. Six days a week, from 8 a.m. to 9 p.m., I worked. Morning meant sweeping the workshop and cleaning the shop with the other workers. Daytime meant learning the craft, sitting over a flame, shaping jewellery for hours without lifting my head. Evening meant staying back at the sales shop, handling customers, and finally locking up, checking the shutters, bolts, and doors again and again out of fear that something would go wrong.

The shift from school to this life was brutal. My teachers, who once praised me, would stop me on the street and ask why I wasn't studying. Their questions weren't meant to hurt, but each one felt like a reminder of what I had lost, of what I could have been.

And inside me, something broke a little.

I felt left behind.

Unlucky.

Different from everyone my age.

Like my life had suddenly taken a path I never chose.

Those early feelings of unfairness turned into emotional

struggle, resentment, sadness, confusion, and a growing sense that life had robbed me of something important. I didn't know how to express it, so I carried it silently, letting it sink deeper into my mind.

Slowly, my thoughts started becoming louder and more persistent. I began overthinking everything, every decision, every mistake, every imagined future. Intrusive thoughts appeared out of nowhere. I started ruminating for hours, replaying the same worries on a loop. I felt different from my friends, different from my family, different from the boy I used to be. And yet no one could see it happening.

The long working hours and sudden change in life began shaping my personality. I became rigid, withdrawn, and overly serious. Work became my identity, not by choice but by force. I didn't have goals anymore. I didn't have a social life. I didn't even know who I was becoming.

Alongside this emotional chaos, the early signs of obsessive-compulsive disorder (OCD) began to appear. I didn't call it OCD then. I didn't even know the term. But the symptoms were very real. I would lock the sales shop and feel the need to check it again, and again, and again.

Something inside me didn't trust my own actions. A voice whispered, "What if it's not locked properly? What if something happens and it's your fault?" So I checked the shutter, the lock, the sliding door, the bolts, sometimes ten times in a row. Only then could I walk away, and even then, uneasily.

Other compulsions began to creep in as well. I would wash my hands repeatedly, not because they were dirty, but because some invisible "impurity" lingered in my mind. I felt a constant need to align objects perfectly, tools on the workbench, jewellery pieces in their trays, even the position of the chairs in the shop, because if something was out of place, I feared disaster or failure.

I also noticed a need to repeat certain phrases silently in my head. Words of reassurance, like "It's okay, it's safe, I did it right," had to be repeated over and over until some faint sense of relief arrived. Otherwise, I felt as though I had invited harm or misfortune.

Even counting became a ritual. I would count steps as I walked through the shop, or the number of items on a tray, convinced that a wrong number could bring bad luck. Sometimes I would repeat small actions, like picking up a tool and putting it down again, until it felt right.

These rituals, small as they seemed, became a way to try to calm the storm inside. But no matter how many times I checked, washed, rearranged, or counted, the unease never fully disappeared. It was a restless loop that quietly took over my mind, leaving me drained and anxious at the end of every day.

Bit by bit, my mind became a place I couldn't escape. Jealousy, insecurity, and intimidation crept in. Seeing my friends move forward while I felt stuck made everything heavier. The comparisons, the doubts, and the fear of failure all fed the invisible prison that was slowly forming around me.

This phase of my life was the beginning of a mind that wouldn't stop. The beginning of restlessness that looked invisible from the outside. The beginning of cracks that would grow deeper before they ever began to heal.

But the truth is, those cracks didn't stay small. They widened. They deepened. And soon, they became the place where I got lost.

Somewhere in that overwhelming phase of life, I stopped recognising myself. It felt like I had fallen into a dark space inside my own mind, a place where I didn't fully exist anymore. I was present on the outside, working, moving, responding, but inside, I felt empty, numb, and disconnected from everything that once made sense.

The OCD, the ruminations, and the constant overthinking drained me completely. They didn't just exhaust my mind. They took away my identity, my confidence, and my sense of being grounded in the world.

I became irritated all the time. The smallest things triggered reactions far bigger than the situation. There were days when just seeing tomatoes in my curry, a food I disliked, would overwhelm me to the point where I'd throw the entire plate away. It wasn't about the food. It was the storm inside me looking for an outlet.

At home, the pressure felt even heavier. I would sometimes spill tea on the floor on purpose, almost as if I needed something outside me to break, because everything inside me already felt shattered. It was a strange release, destructive, but momentarily relieving.

My mother watched all of this with a heart that was breaking quietly. She saw the sudden changes, the irritability, the sadness I couldn't explain, the way I sat alone for hours staring at nothing. She didn't have the language for what was happening inside me, but she could feel her son slipping away into a place she couldn't reach.

There were moments when the suffering felt so unbearable, so suffocating, that I said things I didn't fully understand. I would tell her that I didn't want to live anymore. That maybe ending everything would finally make the pain stop. Maybe it would be easier for everyone if I weren't here.

I didn't want to die. I wanted the suffering to stop. I wanted silence. I wanted my mind back. But at that age, all I knew was that the pain inside me felt bigger than me.

And saying those words, threatening to take my own life, was my desperate attempt to express a level of suffering I didn't know how to put into sentences.

My mother would sit beside me, helpless, terrified, holding her tears back because she didn't want to make things worse. She tried to comfort me, tried to talk me down, tried to pull me out of the darkness with the only tool she had: her love. But even she couldn't reach the parts of my mind that had begun collapsing in on themselves.

At that time, neither I nor my parents were aware of anything like therapy or professional help. We were living in a village where access was limited, and there was also a social stigma around such things. Even the thought of it being exposed carried its own fear.

I started spending more and more time alone. I avoided friends because I couldn't relate to their happiness or goals. I avoided conversations because I feared breaking down or revealing how hollow I felt inside. I avoided myself most of all, because looking at myself felt painful.

I wasn't the bright student anymore. I wasn't the curious teenager with dreams. I wasn't even a hardworking apprentice learning a skill. I felt like a shadow, a version of me with no spark, no direction, and no sense of belonging.

The invisible prison that had begun building years earlier—this is when I first felt myself fully trapped inside it. I didn't know it then, but this was the beginning of a long journey, one that would nearly break me before it began to heal me.

After two years of working, when I turned nineteen, a silent war began inside my mind. I kept asking myself: What am I doing? Where is my life going? Is this all there is for me?

Eventually, something inside me shifted. I realised a truth that felt both frightening and empowering: I was the author of my own life. I could shape it, or I could let it collapse even further. For the first time in years, I felt a spark of control, a small but real sense of direction returning to me.

With that determination, I went to my father and told him what I had decided. I wanted to quit the apprenticeship and go back to studying. My family did not take it well. They had a clear plan for me: finish the apprenticeship, take a small loan, and start my own jewellery business. My father was respected in the community and could easily help me find customers. To them, walking away from that path felt foolish, almost irresponsible.

But deep inside, I knew I couldn't stay in that workshop forever. I wanted to study again, even though the thought of returning to the same system where I once felt trapped terrified me. Still, the alternative, staying stuck, felt worse. So for the first time, I went against my family's expectations.

I decided to go overseas. With a loan my father bravely took on, and with sponsorship help from my aunt and uncle in Canada, who treated me like their own son, for which I am deeply grateful, I was able to secure an Australian student visa in 2007.

That moment was huge for me. It was like the first real crack in the walls of my invisible prison. For the first time in a very long time, I felt a faint but undeniable flicker of hope. A feeling that maybe, just maybe, my life wasn't completely controlled by circumstances. Maybe I could reach for something more.

It was small, fragile, and uncertain, but it was mine.

The first few years in Australia were far from easy. Life as an international student came with challenges I had never imagined: loneliness, fear, financial pressure, and the constant struggle to survive in a foreign country. But slowly, through the difficulties, tiny victories began to appear. Small achievements. Little moments of growth. First steps toward becoming someone I had never believed I could be.

As I settled into student life in Australia, my world slowly began to expand. For the first time, I was surrounded by people from different countries, cultures, traditions, and beliefs. In classrooms and study sessions, we often opened up about our struggles, dreams, and the reasons that brought us across the world.

Among them, I grew close to a few Catholic friends. They were warm, open-hearted, and genuinely curious about my background. Until then, I had barely interacted with anyone from a different faith. My upbringing had been surrounded by Sikh and Hindu influences, so stepping into conversations about Christianity felt both new and strangely comforting.

They often shared parts of their lives with me. Stories of their families, the challenges they faced, and how their faith helped them cope with stress and uncertainty. During one of those conversations, they spoke about something that caught my attention: the forgiveness of sins, unconditional love, the promise of hope and eternal life through Jesus Christ, and the belief that Jesus is the only way to heaven.

It wasn't a debate. It wasn't an attempt to convert me. It was simply friends sharing the source of their strength. Their sincerity touched me.

Eventually, they invited me to a Catholic church. I respected their invitation, but I never made it. Even though I didn't attend, I still listened whenever they shared things about their faith.

They also talked about the Bible. Verses about hope, redemption, compassion, and the idea that a person could start again, no matter how broken they felt inside. At that time, I wasn't sure what I believed. But something about those ideas drew me in. The thought that no matter how many mistakes someone made, they could still be forgiven, still have a fresh beginning, felt incredibly powerful.

For a boy who had spent years trapped inside his own mind, wrestling with guilt, fear, and intrusive thoughts, that message hit deep.

These conversations didn't change my life overnight. But they planted a small seed inside me. A curiosity, a subtle sense of relief, and an understanding that there were perspectives beyond the world I grew up in. It made me want to know more about the Christian faith.

In a foreign land where loneliness often echoed louder than my own thoughts, those friendships became another small crack in the walls of the invisible prison I had been trying so desperately to escape.

But after our graduation, everyone went their own way. Life scattered us in different directions. And once again, things began to decay inside me. Loneliness crept back in, along with the intrusive thoughts and overthinking I thought I had left behind.

Through all those years of struggle, something else shaped my journey quietly. I had never experienced real love.

While people my age were dating and building relationships, I was busy fighting battles inside my own mind. My life was filled with survival, overthinking, loneliness, and trying to hold myself together.

There was no space for romance, no emotional capacity to love or be loved. I often wondered if something was wrong with me, or if love simply wasn't meant for someone like me.

I watched others fall into relationships effortlessly, but I remained untouched by that feeling. It was as if love existed in a different universe, far away from the storms that lived inside me.

I had no idea that one day, a gentle and kind girl would enter my life. Someone whose warmth and care could soften the iron rod I had become. Someone who would stand by me in my struggles and walk with me as I emerged from the invisible prison. Someone loving, caring, loyal, and faithful. Someone wonderful who would help me grow into a good husband and father.

4

Love Arrived From Another World

After graduating in 2009, my focus was simple but enormous. I needed a pathway to permanent residency in Australia. I loved this country. The people of Australia are amazing, friendly, and welcoming. It was the place where I began to stand on my own feet, become independent, and discover who I was without background noise.

Around that time, technology was expanding rapidly. Social media was becoming popular, and the online world suddenly felt huge, alive, and unpredictable.

One ordinary day, I came across a girl online, someone I had never met before. But the moment I saw her picture, something inside me shifted.

It felt like love at first sight, a feeling I had never experienced before. My heart, which had always been quiet, actually beat in a way I had never felt. She was from the Philippines.

We started talking, slowly and naturally. Conversations about life, culture, our days, and our experiences. We always spoke with respect and decency. Nothing forced, nothing dramatic. Just two people connecting through a screen.

Our friendship lasted almost a year, and during that time, something unexpected happened. My heart kept falling for her.

But my mind fought back. It reminded me of everything:

Long-distance doesn't work.

Your life is unstable.

You're desperate and broken.

This can't happen.

I had tasted ruin, and I didn't believe someone like me could love or be loved. But the heart doesn't follow logic.

On May 4, 2010, I couldn't hold it in anymore. I confessed my feelings to her. I told her what my heart had been whispering for months.

She took time to think, and that night felt endless. Then, on May 5, 2010, she said yes. That day, my heart found its reason to beat.

Though we were separated by thousands of miles and different time zones, our connection never wavered. Not a single day went by without us talking. Messages, calls, and small updates about our lives became threads that slowly wove our hearts closer together.

Our love began to grow quietly and steadily. The feelings were undeniable. It felt as though we were meant for each other, two souls finding rhythm across distance.

I began to smile more often. Days that once felt grey and heavy started to fill with colour. My feet felt lighter, as if they had wings. Life, which had once been a series of struggles and survival, began to feel meaningful. I realised that in her love, I felt alive.

After three months, she asked me something that would change the course of our journey.

She told me she loved me deeply, but there was something I had not expected. She was a member of Iglesia ni Cristo, the Church of Christ in the Philippines. We had never really talked about religion before. All she knew was that I was Hindu and Sikh. I knew she was Christian, but she had not shared much about her faith, the Bible, or church teachings.

According to her church's beliefs, salvation could only be found within the church, and membership had to be maintained to remain saved. She could not marry a non-member. If she did, it would not just be a personal choice. It would be a serious violation of church doctrine. She could be expelled, which in their belief meant losing salvation and eventually facing eternal punishment.

It was not only she who would face consequences. Even her parents, who were devoted members, could lose their standing and duties in the church. For them, faith was not just a part of life. It was everything. Obedience came before anything else.

At that time, I did not fully understand the weight of this teaching. I only knew that her church did not allow members to marry outside it, and that breaking this rule could have serious consequences for her and her family.

Some of the strict teachings of Iglesia ni Cristo, whose violation could put salvation at risk, included:

- Failing to attend worship services regularly, often twice a week
- Questioning or doubting the teachings of the church
- Speaking against church leaders or decisions
- Marrying or being involved with a non-member
- Repeatedly breaking church rules
- Disobedience to church expectations

- Failing to participate in church activities
- Not contributing to church funds or projects
- Associating with expelled members
- Ignoring moral and ethical expectations

It was only years later, after carrying the weight of that decision, that I realised how much fear and responsibility this belief had placed on me.

Looking back, I can see that it was one of the forces that strengthened the walls of the invisible prison in my mind. It shaped my doubts and created a fear of losing salvation and facing eternal punishment.

It pushed me into constant overthinking. I felt the need to do everything I could to stay aligned, both mentally and practically. This included regular offerings, following instructions without question, attending services twice a week, and trying to meet every expectation. All of it slowly reinforced the feeling of being trapped.

When she asked me to consider joining her religion, I realised this was not a simple request. It carried serious consequences, including eternal ones, if I ignored it.

At the same time, she loved me. She asked me to consider joining her faith, not as a demand, but as an act of love. For her, for us, and for the future she believed in.

At first, I was stunned. My mind shook again, as if the invisible cracks in my thoughts had reopened. Why had this happened? Why now? I could not leave her, but the path she was asking me to take was not easy.

I had never held a Bible, never attended a church, and knew almost nothing about Christian teachings. Overthinking crept in immediately. Why had she not asked me this from the beginning? Why now, when I was already so invested in her love?

But I could not ignore my heart. I loved her too much, and I could see clearly how much she loved me. Our relationship grew stronger every day, deepening in ways I had never imagined. I realised that if I truly wanted to be with her, I would have to take this step, for love and for us.

It reminded me of the conversations I had years ago with my classmates in Australia, when they shared stories about faith, hope, and the Bible. At the time, I had been curious, and I had felt a quiet pull toward something beyond myself. Perhaps this was not a coincidence. Perhaps it was a gentle nudge guiding me toward this choice.

So I said yes, not fully knowing what it would involve, and not committing to a final decision, but opening myself to try at the right time. That small yes brought her joy, a light that seemed to reach across the distance between us.

As we continued talking daily, she remained patient but persistent. She began searching for a church near me, congregations about 35 kilometres away, so I could attend and learn step by step. Slowly, a new journey began, not just of love, but of faith, understanding, and discovering a world I had never known before.

I began attending regular worship services twice a week, taking part in other church activities, and gradually getting to know the members. Most of the members were Filipino, and I was the only Indian among them. They were curious and welcoming, asking how and why I had come.

For six months, I became deeply passionate and dedicated. I wanted to understand their faith fully, so I would even travel at night to the minister's house to attend Bible teachings and study the church's doctrines.

Many of the members appreciated my sincere effort and determination. They were extremely friendly, helpful, and welcoming, which made it easier for me to feel part of the community. They could see that I was genuinely committed. Yet, as with any new journey, a few began to doubt me, wondering if I was being genuine or just pretending. Their skepticism only made me more determined to learn and prove my sincerity through my actions.

In November 2010, I finally flew to the Philippines to meet my love in person for the first time. After months of talking online, seeing her face-to-face was overwhelming. She was even more beautiful and wonderful than I had imagined, and every moment we spent together made me realise just how real and powerful our connection had become.

I spent nearly three weeks with her, enjoying our time together and having a peaceful break. She introduced me to her family. I had gone to the Philippines without telling my parents in India because I was afraid they would not agree. Their traditions and expectations felt like they would stand in the way of the decision I had made for my own happiness.

During those days, I began to notice something remarkable about her. She did not talk much about her church or its teachings, nor did she quote Bible verses or focus on earning salvation or worrying about losing it. Instead, she simply lived in a way that caught my attention. She was calm, present, kind, grateful, and free from unnecessary worry. She lived in the moment, not trapped in the past or chasing the future.

She moved through each day with a light and peaceful mind, quietly observing life as it came. It amazed me, though at that time I did not fully understand it. I only knew there was a clear difference between her mind and mine, and that curiosity planted a seed in me. Why was her mind so peaceful while mine felt so restless?

Before I left the Philippines, she asked me to secure our relationship. I proposed to her, and with the presence and blessing of her mother, we got engaged.

Somehow, through a few family members on social media, my parents and relatives in India discovered that I had gone to the Philippines to meet the girl I loved. Their reaction was shock and disbelief. What I had done went against every expectation, tradition, and cultural norm they held, and I was the first in my family to take such a step. I was pressured to break up, and at times it felt like I might be cut off from the family I had grown up with.

The distance that grew between us caused deep mental and emotional suffering. On one side, I felt the heavy weight of religious pressure, and on the other, the expectations of family. I was trapped between two worlds. Yet despite the fear, the judgment, and the uncertainty, I chose to remain steadfast in my love. That choice was both terrifying and liberating, and it shaped the path I had to walk.

I was able to secure all of my documents to apply for permanent residency, and gradually, life began to stabilise. I found steady work, and at the same time, I continued to grow stronger in my love and in my faith within the church. Each step forward gave me more confidence and a sense of purpose.

My love for her grew stronger with each passing day. Even though we were in a long-distance relationship, I began to feel as though I could not live without her. She was my first love, my first relationship, and the sacrifices I had made only deepened my attachment. Over time, I became clingy and overly dependent on her presence and attention.

Looking back, I realise that this intense attachment and possessiveness became a source of suffering. Later chapters will explore how this over-attachment created inner turmoil and mental struggle. It was only through learning and applying Buddhist wisdom that I began to see clearly how attachment leads to suffering.

Buddhist teachings helped me understand that clinging and possessiveness are not true forms of love. When we hold on too tightly and try to control someone, love becomes a source of pain for both ourselves and the other person. True love, as I came to understand, is freely given. It does not demand, control, or confine. It accepts the other person as they are, without conditions or expectations. When love is free, it allows both people to grow and find peace together.

In March 2011, I was baptised and officially became a member of the church. Later that year, in September 2011, we got married in the Church of Christ in the Philippines, with the blessing of my parents in India. We visited India in October 2012, and in July 2013, our first son was born in the Philippines. In October 2013, I received my permanent residency in Australia, and in December 2014, my wife and son joined me there. From that point on, we were together, building our life as a family.

I continued to grow stronger in my faith within the church. I was given responsibilities and duties, and eventually became an officer, becoming a very active member. Despite this, I was not encouraged to read the Bible on my own. In fact, it was discouraged. According to church teachings, the full understanding of scripture was considered a mystery reserved only for the leaders. Members were told that interpreting it on their own could lead them away from the truth.

This teaching made me quietly reexamine things. I knew that if I spoke openly about my doubts, I could be expelled, and it could even affect my relationship with my wife. Over time, after a couple of years, I began reading the Bible on my own. Slowly, I started to love the scriptures and immerse myself in them, but once again, I felt a sense of attachment, this time to the Bible itself.

As I continued studying, I began to question the teachings and doctrines of Iglesia ni Cristo that I had been given. When I read the Bible for myself, many of their interpretations seemed taken out of context in the scriptures. I started to feel spiritually dry. I felt less of the presence of God and the Spirit in the church, and more pressure and fear during worship services. At times, I would sit there physically present, but inwardly restless and unsettled, as if something inside me was quietly breaking.

That shift unsettled me deeply. Something no longer felt right, but I could not fully understand why. I continued quietly, researching and reflecting, and still found genuine joy in discovering the scriptures on my own. At the same time, an inner conflict was building, one that I could not ignore. It felt like I was being pulled in two directions, one by fear, and the other by a quiet search for truth. I didn't realise then that life was about to bring a challenge that would shake everything even further.

5

When the World Turned Upside Down

Just as I had begun to quietly explore my own understanding of the scriptures, life brought a challenge I could never have anticipated. In July 2017, we were blessed with our second son in Australia. What should have been a moment of pure joy quickly turned into a moment of unimaginable fear. During the newborn screening, we learned that our son had a rare form of hypothyroidism. He was born without a functioning thyroid gland and would require medication for the rest of his life.

The tests revealed more complications. His jaundice levels had risen dangerously high, and it was confirmed that he had suffered brain damage in the areas controlling movement and motor skills. In that moment, my world felt shattered. I could barely understand the medical terms, the diagnoses, or the lifelong challenges my son might face. The weight of uncertainty and helplessness pressed heavily on me, forcing me to face a reality far harsher than anything I had imagined.

Overthinking, fear, and anxiety began to take over my mind in new and intense ways. My thoughts were constantly consumed by what might happen to my son. Medical terms like cerebral palsy, hearing loss, and developmental delays echoed endlessly in my head. I worried about the long-term effects of thyroid medication, the constant blood tests, repeated hearing checks, and the ongoing cycle of occupational therapy and physiotherapy that lay ahead.

Slowly, I felt defeated. I became trapped in my own mind, overwhelmed by fear and uncertainty. I forgot how to live in the present moment. I forgot how to stay grounded within myself. It felt as though the ground beneath me had disappeared, leaving me lost and exhausted inside my own invisible prison.

At the same time, the question of where I should turn for prayer and healing only added to my struggle. I could no longer fully accept the teachings of Iglesia ni Cristo or feel the presence of God there as I once had. Instead of comfort, I felt confusion and inner conflict.

As time passed, my mind began to unravel. I felt lost, unable to focus, think clearly, or make sense of anything. Fear and overthinking consumed me, and there were moments when I simply wanted everything to end.

With the support of the hospital and medical professionals, therapy began for my son. While his treatment moved forward, I found myself becoming spiritually dry and empty. What amazed me most during this time was my wife. She remained calm, peaceful, and hopeful in the middle of the storm. She stayed grounded in the present moment, quietly hoping for the best possible outcome. Her strength deeply moved me.

With continued support from the hospital and allied health professionals, support I will always be grateful for, our son slowly began to reach his milestones. Although he was behind in some areas for his age, serious conditions such as cerebral palsy and hearing loss were eventually ruled out. Despite the early diagnosis of brain damage, he began to stand and walk slowly by the age of one. Those small steps brought quiet drops of hope and joy back into my life.

During this time, I realised I could no longer confine myself within the church. I began asking questions openly in gatherings, fully aware that I was placing myself at risk of expulsion. A church leader advised me to write a letter of apology, but instead, I handed in my resignation. In that moment, I felt a sense of freedom. Yet my love for the Bible remained, and my search for truth continued.

After leaving the church, a quiet depression settled in. Even though I had stepped away, a lingering fear followed me. The fear of hell, of judgment, of having made an irreversible mistake. That fear did not stay within me. It slowly began to affect my marriage as well. We were both carrying our own burdens, yet our main focus remained on our son. Strangely, the trials we faced did not break our family apart. Instead, they brought us closer together in ways I had not expected.

In the silence that followed my departure from the church, I found myself in a strange spiritual space. What I had once been deeply passionate about now felt unfamiliar, even uncomfortable. My faith, which had once given me certainty, now left me with mixed emotions and unanswered questions. I felt caught between belief and doubt, longing and fear, unsure of which path to follow. At that time, I did not realise that this confusion was not the end of my journey, but the beginning of a deeper and more honest awakening.

As my son began to reach his milestones, and in some areas even exceeded expectations according to medical assessments, another shift quietly took place. Friends and brethren from the church started to distance themselves from me. Some unfriended me on social media, while others withdrew without explanation. A few went further, treating me with quiet judgment, as though my questions had marked me as someone to be avoided.

At the same time, there were others who showed concern in their own way. Some reached out, encouraging me to return, believing they were helping me find my way back. Their intentions were not always unkind, but the pressure was heavy. What I needed most during that time was understanding and space to heal. Instead, I found myself once again caught between care and expectation. This experience deepened my inner conflict and slowly shaped the path I was being led toward, one that would eventually teach me the difference between fear-based belonging and genuine freedom.

I began reading the Bible more often, immersing myself in the scriptures and noticing more and more inconsistencies in the church's teachings. Though I hesitated at first, I felt a growing need to share what I was discovering with my wife. I was fully aware at that time of how her mind had been conditioned and programmed by the church's teachings, doctrines, and the fear that if she were expelled, she would lose her salvation. I also knew that the blame could fall on my shoulders, and that she might face persecution from her family and other church members.

At times, these conversations were not easy, as they challenged beliefs we had both held for years, especially for her, as she was born and raised in the church. There were moments of uncertainty, questions without immediate answers, and a quiet fear of where this path might lead. Yet, deep within, there was also a sense that we were moving closer to something real and honest. Instead of forcing conclusions, we allowed space for reflection, trusting the process as it unfolded.

Over months of careful conversations, sharing scriptures, and gentle guidance, she gradually came to see things more clearly. Eventually, she made the courageous decision to resign from her membership in Iglesia ni Cristo. It was not a decision made lightly, nor was it made for me, but one that came after much thought, prayer, and inner wrestling. In that moment, I saw not only her courage, but also her commitment to truth, no matter the cost.

Living in truth brought us clarity and the freedom to embrace a life guided by genuine love and faith, rather than fear or obligation. It allowed us to step out of fear-based thinking, especially the fear of going to hell after leaving the church.

6

Chasing God Everywhere

After stepping away from Iglesia ni Cristo and embracing truth for myself and my wife, I found myself in unfamiliar spiritual territory. I no longer felt bound by fear or obligation, yet I was restless and searching. Who was God beyond the teachings I had been given? Where could I find guidance, peace, and understanding that felt real? Where could I encounter the God of the Bible, and which church, if any, should I turn to now?

My love and attachment to the God of the Bible and the scriptures began to grow, becoming an important part of my life. I also started to reflect deeply on what it truly means to be saved. Was salvation only about being part of a particular church, or was it about knowing God personally and living in truth and faith? These questions pushed me to look deeper, beyond rituals and fear, and to seek a relationship with God that felt genuine and free.

During this time of searching, the husband of a Filipino friend of my wife invited me to his church, a Born-Again congregation. I shared my story, my struggles, and my fears about Iglesia ni Cristo. I met the pastor and other members, and at first, it felt welcoming. But what I was told stayed with me. They said Iglesia ni Cristo was a false church, and that I had now come to the "right" one.

Their teachings were very different from what I had known, and at first, I felt relief in the less strict environment. I attended services for several months. But once again, my questions and independent thinking were not welcomed. Eventually, I was quietly pushed away.

Determined to continue searching, I attended another church of a different denomination. The same pattern repeated. They told me that Born-Again churches were not the true church, and that I had now come to the "right" place. Once again, my curiosity and desire to understand things for myself were not accepted, and I could not stay.

Later, I met a security officer at one of my work sites. He was an ex-Catholic who had embraced Islam and become a practicing Muslim. We had many conversations about religion and faith. Gradually, I began to lose some confidence in the Bible and became curious about Islam. At first, it seemed structured and clear. But as I learned more, I was told that Christianity was corrupted and that Islam was the only true religion. It felt familiar. Another path claiming to be the only right one. I realised I was again caught in a cycle of being told what to believe.

This pattern continued for almost two years. Everywhere I went, I heard the same message in different forms. Each group claimed to hold the truth. Each said the others were wrong. Each tried to reshape my beliefs and identity.

I found myself chasing God everywhere. Moving from church to church, belief to belief, hoping to find certainty, peace, and truth. Instead, I felt more confused. The more I searched outside, the more lost I became inside. What began as a sincere search slowly turned into exhaustion, doubt, and inner conflict.

Alongside all this searching, something else began to take hold of me, something I did not understand at the time.

I developed intense health anxiety and a deep fear of dying. It started small, but I made a mistake that made everything worse. I began checking my symptoms online. What I thought would reassure me only filled me with fear. Every search led to serious and life-threatening conditions.

From there, a pattern formed.

Almost daily, I would notice sensations in my body. A tightness. A pain. A strange feeling. And my mind would jump straight to the worst possible conclusion. I would search again and again, looking for reassurance. But instead of calming me, it made everything worse.

The thoughts became constant. Obsessive. Uncontrollable.

Fear of death, fear of serious illness, and even fear of neurological disorders took over my mind. I couldn't switch it off. The more I tried to find certainty, the more uncertain and afraid I became.

It reached a point where I was visiting doctors repeatedly, sometimes multiple times a day. Going from one clinic to another, hoping someone would finally tell me I was okay. But the relief never lasted. Within hours, sometimes minutes, the fear returned.

I didn't realise it then, but I was caught in a cycle. A loop of fear, checking, temporary relief, and then fear again.

Years passed, and I became an independent Bible researcher. Something unexpected began to happen. Things I had never heard in any of the churches I attended started to become clear as I read the Bible in context. Step by step, I began believing in and following the commandments, including the Sabbath and dietary laws. Many today would recognise this as Torah observance.

At first, I was not part of any group or movement. I explored on my own, sharing only with my wife. Over time, she also came to believe the same.

Through my research, I discovered something that many churches rarely discuss, said with respect. Israel is central throughout the Bible, yet its role is often misunderstood. Some teachings take verses out of context and form the idea that the Church has replaced Israel.

Encouraged by what I was learning, I began writing and sharing my thoughts online. I was later able to publish my first book, *Fullness of the Gentiles: The Mystery of the Return of Ephraim*, on 24 July 2021. The book received positive reviews on Amazon. It is available on Amazon for those who wish to explore the topic further.

In it, I explained who Israel truly is, drawing directly from scripture. I shared the history of Israel's divided kingdom—the ten northern tribes, known as the house of Israel, scattered among the nations, and the two southern tribes, the house of Judah. I also highlighted Messiah Yeshua's (Jesus) role in restoring both houses. In short, the Bible shows that Israel and the Church are deeply connected, not separate.

Many believers appreciated my research and writing. I was welcomed to join Torah and Hebrew Roots groups and movements. But over time, I noticed patterns of pride, judgment, and toxicity among some Torah-observant believers. Conflicts often arose over the correct calendar for the feasts, the proper names for God and Yeshua, interpretations of scripture, eschatology, how strictly to observe laws, and even outward practices like head coverings or tzitzit (tassels worn on garments as a reminder of the commandments).

Sadly, many of these Torah-observant believers were formerly Christians, yet they were often hostile and judgmental toward Christians, creating an atmosphere of division rather than understanding. Personal opinions frequently became treated as the only correct way, and disagreements could quickly turn into exclusion or criticism.

These experiences pushed me away once again, reminding me that spiritual journeys are not only about discovering truth but also navigating human imperfection along the way. Even when truth is found, the human element can complicate the path, requiring patience, discernment, and a steady heart to continue moving forward. Yet my love for God and the Bible grew stronger, and I continued as an independent Bible researcher, diving ever deeper into scripture to know God directly, without relying on human authority.

7

When Belief Breaks

As the world grappled with COVID and lockdowns stretched on, life slowed down in ways none of us could have expected. For many, the pandemic brought fear, isolation, and uncertainty. For me, it also brought an unexpected gift: time. Time to pause, reflect, and immerse myself in Bible study without distraction.

At the same time, I was still dealing with the turmoil of my own mind. The anxiety, the overthinking, and the constant search for certainty had not left me.

Freed from the toxic environments of churches and Torah-observant groups, I could finally think, research, and question on my own terms.

Years of independent study followed. The deeper I went into scripture, the more I began to doubt teachings I had once held as absolute truth. What if much of what I had been told had overlooked history, context, and prophecy? What if scripture was not mainly a roadmap to the future, but a record of God's dealings with humanity in history? These questions consumed me.

Across different communities, whether Christian, Torah-observant, or Jewish, one idea kept appearing: the "Day of the Lord" is near, and unfulfilled prophecies will happen soon. Many connect this with the second coming of Yeshua (Jesus), often creating urgency and fear. But without proper historical and cultural context, these interpretations can lead to misunderstanding.

I poured these insights into my second book, *Malachi's Elijah Revealed: Neither John Nor the Future Elijah,* published on 22 December 2025. Although I had written it earlier, it was finally released then. In it, I re-examined the Day of the Lord and Malachi's prophecy, returning to its original audience and context to better understand Elijah and challenge common assumptions about the second coming of Jesus.

I also revisited other prophecies in Daniel, Ezekiel, and Isaiah, carefully studying their language and historical setting. Slowly, a different understanding began to form. The Bible appeared more historical than predictive.

But this clarity came at a cost.

Everything I had believed for years now felt uncertain. The beliefs I had held close, the ones tied to my identity and sense of purpose, began to slip away. My mind, already prone to overthinking, went into overdrive. Obsessive thoughts, anxiety, and exhaustion grew stronger.

I began to see something clearly. Suffering comes from clinging. As the Buddha taught, '*From attachment springs grief, from attachment springs fear.*' (**Dhammapada 212**). I had loved my beliefs, my understanding, and my connection to God more than almost anything else in life. And now, confronted with the unraveling of those attachments, I felt the full weight of loss, confusion, and despair. Years of devotion, study, and effort, all challenged. All questioned.

Yet even in the midst of this turmoil, I did not abandon my search. My love for God and the scriptures remained, even if my previous interpretations had failed me. I continued my study, still independent, still seeking truth directly from the Bible, free from human authority, and this time with a heart prepared to let go of clinging. Every passage I read and every prophecy I revisited, I discovered, was not what mainstream teachings believed.

The world had changed. I had changed. And I realized that the journey of faith is not only about uncovering truth, but also about learning to hold it lightly, to live with uncertainty, yet remain devoted to seeking God with an open, steady heart.

I started to doubt many of the teachings I had long held, especially the widely accepted idea of the second coming of Jesus. I tried to discuss my questions with a few believers and teachers, but I quickly realized how close-minded many were. Their answers felt rigid, defensive, and unyielding.

After years of reading Scripture in context, one question rose above all others: Who was the Bible actually written for? What was the historical and cultural context? Are most people reading it sincerely in context, or just picking verses to fit their beliefs? I began to see that personal belief cannot override truth, and that the pursuit of truth can feel lonely when everyone else seems trapped in assumptions.

Then came the question of other religions. Most people claim their faith is the only true religion, their scripture the only true word of God. If this is the case, where could I go? Which path should I follow? Which scripture should I believe? They all seemed to contradict one another.

I was searching for God, seeking to serve Him, but the more

I looked, the more I found myself standing alone. In every direction, different religions offered different gods, different names for their gods, and different paths to reach Him. For the first time, I felt truly vulnerable, exposed, uncertain, and stripped of the comfort of certainty I had clung to for so many years.

For the first time, I realized that faith could break. Questions I had never dared to ask before began flooding my mind: Did God create us, or did humans create God? Was religion meant to be a medicine for the soul, or had it become a disease? Was it meant to bring clarity, or had it sown confusion? Could all religions be true in their own way, or were they all false?

Were they divinely inspired, or simply constructs of human minds? Why had religion caused so much conflict, so many fights and divisions throughout history? And perhaps the most painful question of all: which religion, if any, had actually made the world a better place to live?

I became spiritually dry. I was confronted with profound loneliness. It was a humbling and painful realization. The more I sought God, the more I saw the limits of human authority, human interpretation, and human certainty. My faith was no longer anchored in what others said, what churches taught, or what leaders claimed.

It was the worst mental pain I had ever encountered. My heart and mind felt shattered. The beliefs I had devoted years to, the teachings I had trusted, and the comfort I had clung to for so long all had lost their footing.

From Sikhism and Hinduism, through Christianity, Torah-observant teachings, and Islam, what I noticed was striking: too often, religion seemed to instill fear, rules, and pressure rather than peace, mindfulness, clarity, or a genuine connection to the Divine. While the scriptures themselves may not directly instill fear, it was the way people, communities, and adherents interpreted and enforced these teachings that often did. There was also a noticeable lack of awareness of ego, which frequently amplified judgment, pride, and control.

Instead of guiding seekers toward compassion, inner strength, and understanding, many teachings emphasized obedience, judgment, or "correct belief," leaving the seeker anxious, confused, or trapped in guilt. This realization made me reflect on how much human influence and unexamined ego can overshadow the original purpose of the scriptures.

I felt more isolated than ever, as if I were standing alone in a vast landscape of doctrines and rules, each pointing in different directions. The very systems I had trusted to bring guidance now highlighted human limitations, pride, and fear. It was humbling to see that the spiritual structures meant to nurture faith could also create anxiety, division, and doubt. In that emptiness, I had no choice but to confront the raw questions of existence, belief, and purpose for myself, without relying on anyone else to provide the answers.

Peace was far from me. There was no clarity, only sadness. The invisible prison had become stronger than ever. My mind kept replaying everything: What happened? Why did this happen? I had been so deeply attached to being religious, to being "right" with God, but that attachment itself became a source of real suffering.

The judgments, arguments, and experiences I had encountered didn't leave me. They followed me. They turned into repetitive mental battles. I found myself arguing with people in my mind, replaying countless conversations and scenarios over and over again. It became an invisible war, one that no one else could see, but one that consumed me daily. Slowly, it began to affect even the smallest parts of my life. Simple daily activities triggered storms of OCD, rumination, and mental pain. I could no longer think clearly.

There were moments when the suffering became so intense that thoughts of ending my life returned.

My wife saw my misery. All she could do was sit beside me, comfort me, and encourage me to start fresh, to let go and move forward. But my mind wouldn't allow it. What confused me even more was seeing her calmness. Her mind remained steady and peaceful, while mine felt like it was collapsing.

I tried again and again to let go, to forget, to move on, but the harder I tried, the worse it became. The more I resisted the intrusive thoughts, the stronger and more frequent they returned. The more I tried to escape them, the more they followed me. The more I suppressed them, the more powerful they came back the next time.

At times, the frustration became physical. I would hit my head, overwhelmed by the noise inside my mind, desperate for silence.

One day, I looked at myself in the mirror and barely recognised who I had become. This wasn't the person I thought I would be. Guilt began to take over. I blamed myself for everything. I felt responsible for my own suffering.

A thought began to settle deep within me: I shouldn't have gone down this path. I shouldn't have tried so hard to become religious.

I became extremely negative. I started noticing faults and imperfections in everyone around me, people who made mistakes, even minor ones, and everyday behaviours that didn't meet my expectations. Sadly, this extended to my wife, who is kind, patient, and truly wonderful. I found myself fixating on her mistakes and imperfections, allowing them to irritate and frustrate both her and me, instead of appreciating the love, care, and support she gave me every single day.

There were times when my behaviour affected her deeply, yet she never wavered. Her love remained steady, even when I failed to see it. In my darkest moments, overwhelmed by mental suffering, I told her, "I have become an animal, not a human. You can leave me and live your life."

Her answer surprised me and cut through the despair: "I respect my wedding vows. I will be with you in good times and in bad times."

Seeing her mindset, her calmness, her patience, and her kindness gave me a glimpse of what was possible. I wanted to change, but I didn't yet know how. I began observing her closely, trying to understand why her mind remained so steady and unreactive, why she could be patient and kind while I was consumed by chaos and negativity. Her example became a mirror, showing me a path I had never fully considered.

I realised that this was the true strength of my wife. She was like a pure, open sky, calm and steady, while storms, clouds, and harsh weather of life passed through without disturbing her essence. No matter the chaos around her, her mind remained clear, peaceful, and unwavering. Watching her, I began to understand that this steadiness was not weakness or indifference, but a quiet, powerful strength that could endure every trial without losing its clarity.

Interestingly, my wife was not deeply religious by choice. Her faith was inherited, part of the religion she was born into. Yet her qualities went beyond any religious requirement. Her calmness, patience, and kindness existed independently of ritual, doctrine, or obligation. It became clear to me that true spiritual strength and steadiness were not rooted in strict religiosity, but in the way the mind was trained, observed, and guided.

From all of this, I learned one crucial thing: the problem was not with any religion, with other people, or with the circumstances around me. The problem was with my own mind. I had never truly understood it, never observed how it reacts, clings, and suffers. Everything, my fear, my despair, my negativity, came from an untrained mind. In short, my mind was untrained.

This realisation marked the beginning of a new journey, learning to understand, calm, and guide my own mind.

What I did not realise at that time was that this breaking point was not the end of my journey, but the beginning of something entirely new. As my beliefs collapsed and my mind reached its limits, I was unknowingly being led toward a different kind of understanding, one that was not built on fear, identity, or external authority, but on direct observation and inner clarity.

I did not have the answers yet. I was still lost, still searching, still hurting. But something had shifted within me. For the first time, instead of trying to fix the world, religion, or other people, I began to turn inward, toward the mind itself.

8

When I Met a Monk

By this stage in my life, something had already begun to shift within me. As I continued observing my wife and her mindset, I started to look more closely at the people around me. What I noticed shocked me. Almost everyone I spoke to carried some form of mental struggle. Anxiety, overthinking, depression, OCD — these were not rare conditions, but common experiences. Even within my own family in India, some had been silently dealing with these struggles for years.

What surprised me even more was how little people spoke about it. So much suffering, yet so much silence. No one openly addressed it. No one seemed to fully understand it or seek a deeper solution. This stirred something within me. I began questioning again: Why do people suffer mentally? Why do some minds remain calm, like my wife's, while others are constantly restless and trapped?

This time, my search was different. I was no longer driven by fear, obsession, or the need to fix myself. Instead, there was a quiet curiosity, a sincere desire to understand the mind itself. In that search, I came across something unexpected. I discovered that Buddhist monks seemed to carry the same qualities I had seen in my wife: calmness, clarity, patience, and a non-reactive mind.

At first, I had to laugh at myself. There was a time when I looked down on Buddhist monks. During my years of trying to be religious in churches and Torah groups, I had dismissed them in my mind. I saw them as people who had withdrawn from life, detached from the opportunities and beauty of the world. All I had ever been taught in mainstream religions was to strive for something beyond this life, heaven as the ultimate goal.

Because of that, I saw Buddhist monks and Buddhist practices as nothing more than a philosophy that missed the point of life. Looking back, I realised how limited and conditioned my thinking had been. What I once ignored, even dismissed, was now standing right in front of me, quietly offering something I had been searching for all along.

I found a Buddhist monastery and, without informing anyone, I went there just to see, hoping I might get a chance to speak with a monk. To my surprise, I was able to meet one. I introduced myself, and the monk respectfully allowed me to sit and talk. I was there for around an hour and a half, accompanied by my wife and two children. The monk listened patiently as I poured out my story, never interrupting, never judging. Tea was offered, and as we sipped, he said something simple yet profound:

"*When you sip tea, that sip is gone. You cannot get it back. You can only take a new sip.*" This is impermanence.

At first, I didn't understand. He explained that life is like this: everything is impermanent. Nothing lasts forever. But people often give impermanent things a fixed meaning, and that is what creates conflict and suffering within us. I smiled quietly, thinking of my life. All I had been taught in religion was to strive for eternity, to cling to membership, duties, commandments, and rituals as a guaranteed path to heaven, things that would never change.

The monk continued. He explained that the root cause of suffering is clinging to what is past or subject to change. I was holding onto my past, and even the pasts of others, and trying to make them permanent. That is why my mind had been trapped in endless struggle.

He gave another example. Imagine seeing someone driving a very expensive car. Your mind immediately thinks, "They must be rich. I want that too." Stories, judgments, and desires are created by the mind. But if someone from a remote tribe saw that car, they might not even know what it is. The problem is not the car, nor the person who owns it, nor even the tribe, but the craving and attachment your mind creates. This, he said, is another root of suffering.

Then he shared another insight. There is no fixed self. I was dwelling on the past, my wife's past, other people's past, my own past, but none of it truly belongs to me. Even I do not fully "own" myself. Everything is transient. Holding on creates the illusion of ownership and deepens suffering.

In simple terms, what I was calling "my life," "my past," and "my identity" was not something fixed or solid. It was a collection of changing experiences, memories, and thoughts. But my mind was treating it as something permanent, something that had to be protected and held on to. That is where the pain was coming from. The more I tried to hold on, the heavier it became. And the more I believed it was truly "mine," the more deeply I suffered.

He also taught me not to identify with thoughts or emotions. Instead, simply observe them, like clouds passing through the sky. Thoughts may come and go, emotions may rise and fall, but you are not the clouds. You are the sky itself, vast, open, and unchanged. By observing without attachment or judgment, the mind can begin to rest in its natural clarity, free from the storms that usually overwhelm it.

The most remarkable part was this. For the first time in my life, someone from another belief did not ask me to change my religion, adopt a different faith, or condemn other religions. The monk showed respect for all beliefs. Unlike many others who had told me before, "Now you have come to the right path, and other religions are false," the monk said nothing of the sort. Instead, he simply said, "**Be present. Be here now. Discover yourself.**"

I felt a small, light shift in my mind, an unfamiliar sense of clarity and relief. It was a quiet message, but it changed something deep within me.

As my time at the monastery came to an end, the monk mentioned that he would introduce me to a senior monk who could guide me further and help me understand more of the teachings and practices.

A week later, I was given the opportunity to meet this senior monk, who became an important guide in my journey. He patiently taught me walking and sitting meditation, showing me how to centre the mind and observe it without attachment. As he shared his personal story, how he came to become a monk, I was struck by the similarities between his struggles and my own. It was a moment of recognition. I realised that my journey, though different in form, reflected the path he had walked, and his experience offered a light I had long been searching for.

During our time together, he shared wisdom that planted the beginning of a deeper journey within me. One point stayed with me above all else: knowledge alone is not enough. What we learn must be practised; otherwise, it is meaningless. He also explained something that deeply challenged me: you cannot be free from suffering until you truly understand it. Avoiding it, rejecting it, or trying to escape it only keeps it alive. Instead, suffering must be observed, understood, and faced with awareness. In that understanding, he said, there is growth and transformation.

He told me something very simple: don't fight the thoughts. Simply observe them without any identification or interpretation. At first, it felt too simple to matter. But I would later realise that this simplicity was the doorway to everything.

For the first time, I wasn't being told what to believe. I was being shown how to see.

Meditation, he said, is not just a technique. It is an art that requires consistency, patience, and dedication.

Meeting the senior monk marked the beginning of a new phase in my life. A phase less about belief and more about direct experience. Until then, I had been searching for answers in doctrines and teachings, but now I began to see that true understanding comes from practice, observation, and patience.

I knew this would not be easy. Learning to calm the mind, to sit with discomfort, and to observe thoughts without attachment would challenge me deeply. Old patterns of obsession, judgment, and negativity were still strong. I expected failure, frustration, and resistance along the way.

Yet, for the first time in years, I felt a spark of hope. A sense that change was possible, not through external authority or rigid rules, but through patient practice and honest self-observation.

In the chapters ahead, I will share the teachings and practices I learned from the monk, my direct experience, and my reading and understanding of Buddhist wisdom. I will also explore what meditation is, the struggles I faced, and the insights that slowly emerged as I applied this wisdom to my life. This is not a story of instant transformation, but of gradual change, learning, failing, and slowly discovering clarity and peace within the mind.

For me, Buddhist wisdom is not a religion or a philosophy, but a way of seeing life clearly. It did not impose rigid rules. Instead, it offered a practical way of living with awareness, patience, and clarity. It taught me a profound lesson: to accept life as it is, rather than constantly resisting it. For most of my life, I had been taught to strive for a perfect state, something beyond this world that I could never truly reach in this human body. But here, I was learning something different, to understand this moment, this mind, and this life as it is.

More importantly, it introduced me to a path based on direct experience. It shifted my focus away from arguments and beliefs, and toward something far more real: the experience of suffering within myself and the possibility of understanding and transforming it. Instead of asking which belief was right, I began to see that the real question was how to observe, understand, and free the mind from its own patterns. For the first time, I began to see that this understanding could also help with the very struggles that had been consuming me—overthinking, anxiety, and OCD.

II

Understanding the Problem

To find peace, we must first see why the mind feels restless and out of control. This section examines the problem, why thoughts and emotions arise and feel personal, why they stir conflict, and how attachment, craving, and the urge to control create suffering. We also explore how trying to escape these feelings doesn't solve anything; it only masks them, making them stronger. This part isn't about fixing anything. It's about seeing clearly so freedom can begin.

9

Why Thoughts and Emotions Arise

Do you know what thought is passing through your mind right now as you read this?

If you are not fully present, your mind is likely already somewhere else, drifting into a past memory, thinking about something unrelated, or planning what comes next.

Can you tell what your next thought will be?

What about in the next few minutes?

Later tonight, before you sleep?

Or the very first thought when you wake up in the morning?

The honest answer is, we don't know. You experience thousands of thoughts every day, but can you know where they come from? Can you control your thoughts?

Right now, do this with me. Decide your next thought and see what happens. The moment you try to decide your next thought, another thought about trying to decide it appears. It is not something you consciously create. It simply appears.

Try another one. Don't think of a pink elephant for the next 60 seconds and see what happens. The image of a pink elephant will appear in your mind almost instantly.

Or try this: don't think about biting into a fresh lemon. Notice how the image, and even the sensation, appear almost instantly.

The moment you hear this, the mind brings the image up on its own. Even though the instruction is not to think about it, the thought still appears. The more you try to push it away, the more it returns.

This shows something important. Thoughts do not always follow our commands. In fact, the very effort to control a thought can make it appear more strongly. What we try to avoid often becomes the very thing the mind focuses on.

Thoughts arise on their own. They come and go without asking for our permission. Yet we live as if we are in control of them, as if we are the ones creating every thought intentionally.

For most people, the mind feels like a constant stream of noise, thoughts coming one after another, emotions rising and falling without warning. A small situation can trigger anxiety. A memory can bring sadness or depression. A single word from someone can create anger that lingers far longer than it should.

But very few people stop to ask: Why is this happening?

Instead, we try to manage it from the outside. We distract ourselves with work, entertainment, relationships, or even religion. We try to suppress thoughts, control emotions, or replace them with something "better." Yet no matter what we do, they keep returning. The mind does not stay quiet for long.

Understanding where thoughts come from is key to understanding the mental struggles created by thoughts and emotions. In this, we begin to see more clearly how the mind operates.

Thoughts Arise from Conditions

I experienced this deeply in my own life. My mind was constantly active, thinking, analysing, judging, replaying past events, and worrying about the future. Even when everything seemed fine externally, there was unrest internally. I believed the cause was outside, in people, situations, and circumstances. I never questioned the nature of the mind itself.

What I slowly began to see was this: thoughts and emotions arise on their own. They are not something we consciously create. A thought appears, then another, then another. An emotion follows, sometimes instantly, sometimes gradually.

From a Buddhist perspective, these arise due to conditions, our past experiences, habits, memories, and what we take in through our senses. Over time, these conditions form patterns in the mind, shaping how thoughts and emotions arise again and again. As found in the **Samyutta Nikaya**: *"When this is, that is. With the arising of this, that arises; when this ceases, that ceases."*

This means that our thoughts and emotions arise naturally, shaped by conditions, and are not something we fully control. The mind is constantly processing and reacting. As the Buddha also said, *"Mind precedes all mental states. Mind is their chief; they are mind-made"* (**Dhammapada 1–2**).

As taught in the **Vina Sutta**, the Buddha used a simple example. Just as a lute produces sound only when certain conditions come together—the instrument, the strings, the player, and the act of playing—sound does not exist on its own. It arises when these conditions are present, and it fades when they are gone.

In the same way, thoughts and emotions arise when conditions come together. Our past experiences, memories, habits, and what we take in through our senses all play a part. When these conditions meet, a thought appears. When they change, the thought fades.

For example, someone may say something small, and suddenly anger arises. The words themselves may be simple, but they connect with past experiences, expectations, and sensitivities within the mind. Because these conditions are present, the emotion appears. If those conditions were different, the same words might not create any reaction.

In another situation, you may smell a familiar scent, and instantly, a memory from years ago comes to mind. The memory was not there a moment ago, yet it appears clearly. It arises because the scent connects with stored experiences in the mind. When the scent is gone, the memory slowly fades again.

In the same way, when the eyes see something pleasant, desire can arise. When the ears hear something unpleasant, irritation can arise. These reactions do not come from a single source. They arise because of contact, perception, and past conditioning. When these conditions change, the reaction also changes.

Thoughts arise whether you want them or not, as long as the conditions are present. The more you try to fight or suppress a thought, that very reaction becomes another condition. When another thought arises, it meets that condition, and again there is resistance. This process continues and gradually becomes a mental struggle.

Thought is a process, not something fixed or permanent.

Imagine a candle. When the conditions are present, the flame appears. The wax, the wick, and the oxygen come together, and a flame is produced. When these conditions change or are no longer present, the flame goes out. In the same way, thoughts arise depending on conditions and follow patterns shaped by those conditions.

A Simple Way to See It

Thoughts arise from conditions.

If you do not fully control your thoughts, then where are they coming from?

As the Buddha taught in the **Samyutta Nikaya (Nidana Samyutta)**: *"When this exists, that exists. With the arising of this, that arises; when this ceases, that ceases."* Nothing exists on its own. Everything arises from conditions.

Think of something simple, like a reflection in a mirror. A reflection does not appear on its own. It arises only when certain conditions are present—the mirror, the object, and the light. If any of these are missing, there is no reflection. When the conditions change, the reflection disappears.

You can also think of a seed growing into a plant or a tree. A seed on its own does not grow. It needs soil, water, sunlight, and the right environment. When these conditions are present, growth happens. When they are not, nothing grows. The seed does not control its growth. It responds to the conditions around it.

Thoughts and emotions work in the same way.

In simple terms, thoughts and emotions arise because certain conditions are present. When those conditions change, the thoughts and emotions also change.

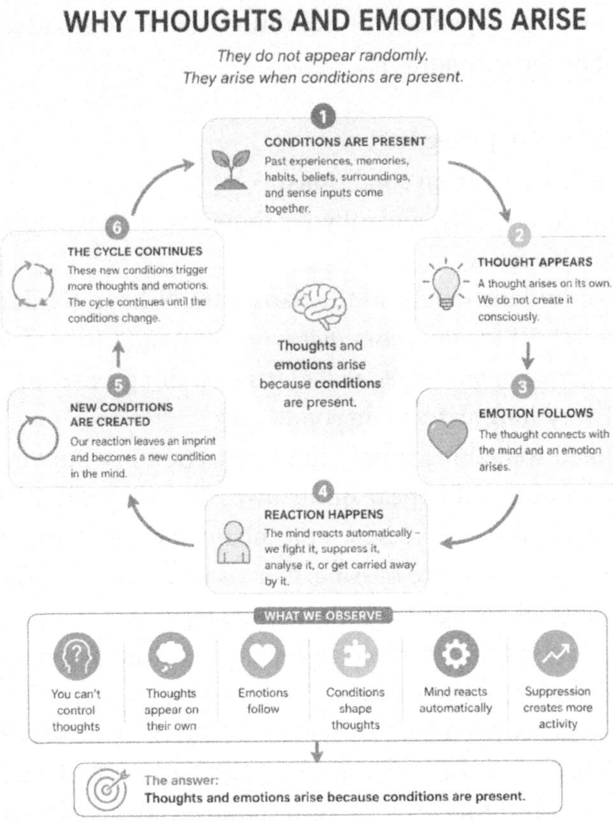

Why Thoughts Become a Struggle

The problem is not that thoughts and emotions exist. The problem is that we identify with them. We say, "I am angry," instead of seeing that anger is arising. We say, "I am anxious," instead of noticing anxiety as a passing state. We treat every thought as truth and every emotion as who we are. In short, we believe we are the owners of every thought and emotion.

We are so quick to claim ownership over thoughts and emotions that we forget they are processes, not instant creations. This identification happens almost automatically. The moment a thought appears, we follow it. The moment an emotion arises, we become it. This is why the mind often feels overwhelming, because instead of observing it, we are lost inside it.

Consider a few everyday examples.

You are lying in bed at night, ready to sleep, and suddenly your mind replays something you said earlier in the day. "Why did I say that?" "That was embarrassing." The body is still, but the mind refuses to rest.

You are about to leave the house, and a thought appears: "What if I left the stove on?" You go back and check. It's off. But as you walk away, the doubt returns, and you feel the need to check again, even though you already know the answer.

You remember a past mistake, and guilt swells: "I shouldn't have done that. I am a failure." Even though the event is long over, the thought and emotion continue to loop.

You plan the day ahead and worry: "What if I fail? What if things go wrong?" Fear and restlessness arise, even before anything has happened.

These examples show that thoughts and emotions arise naturally and are shaped by conditions. They persist because we cling to them, personalise them, and replay them in our minds. The mind reacts almost like a machine, generating one thought after another, one emotion after another, often without awareness.

The key insight here is simple: thoughts and emotions are natural processes of the mind. They arise, remain for a time, and then fade. The difficulty is that most people never notice this. They are caught inside the flow, mistaking these mental events for who they are. It is this identification, this constant ownership, that makes the mind feel restless and overwhelmed.

Imagine this: at work, someone makes a rude or negative comment about you. Almost immediately, a thought arises: "I am hurt. That person has disrespected me in front of others. I cannot accept this." From that single thought, the mind begins to spin a story—an endless sequence of episodes. Since you have identified with the thought and positioned yourself as a character in the story, the mind quickly creates more "players": "I am hurt. That person was wrong. Others were watching. I was insulted. My image is tarnished."

Now the mind works tirelessly to protect this "me" in the story. Every reaction, judgment, and imagined scenario reinforces the sense of ownership over the thought and the emotion. The more you fight it, argue with it, or try to fix it in your mind, the stronger it becomes. Each time you see that person again, the wound reopens, and the same thoughts return, often with even greater intensity.

Meanwhile, the person who made the comment has likely moved on, perhaps enjoying a meal, spending time with friends or family, completely unaware of the storm their words have created in your mind.

You, however, remain restless. The thoughts replay for hours, days, or even weeks. The one who is hurt continues to suffer, while the one who caused the pain may be completely at peace. Why? Because you have claimed ownership of the thought and the suffering it generates. You have personalised it, made it yours, and turned a moment into something permanent.

If we look at this more deeply, something very important

becomes clear. The person who made the rude comment is not necessarily a "bad" person. They may have spoken out of their own stress, habits, or lack of awareness. That single moment does not define them, just as it does not need to define you. The event itself was brief. It happened and passed. It was impermanent.

But the mind does not see it this way. It holds on, repeats, and builds upon it, creating layers of meaning and illusion. This is how an untrained mind works, and I have experienced this same cycle, this same quiet suffering of thought and emotion, again and again.

Consider another common scenario: you see a friend post a photo of an exciting vacation on social media. Almost immediately, a thought arises: "Why didn't I get to go there? Why am I not as successful or happy as they are?" From that single thought, the mind begins to spin a story: "I've worked so hard, yet I'm not where I want to be. People must be judging me. I'm falling behind. I'll never catch up."

Once again, the moment you identify with the thought, you place yourself inside the story. The mind quickly creates more "players": the "successful friend," the "judging world," and "me, the one who is lacking." Each thought strengthens the narrative, and the mind begins to replay it, compare, analyse, and imagine different outcomes.

Now the mind works to protect this image of "me." It keeps comparing, measuring, and reinforcing the feeling of lack. The more you engage with these thoughts, the deeper the sense of dissatisfaction grows. Each time you see similar posts or think about your life, the same pattern repeats, often becoming stronger.

Meanwhile, your friend is simply enjoying their moment,

present, relaxed, and unaware of the storm their photo has created in your mind.

You, however, may feel restless and unsettled. The thoughts return again and again, not because of the photo itself, but because of the meaning your mind has attached to it. A simple image has now turned into a story of comparison, self-doubt, and inadequacy.

If we look more closely, something important becomes clear. The photo itself is neutral. It is just a moment captured and shared. Your friend's happiness does not take anything away from you, nor does it define your worth. The feeling of lack did not come from the photo. It arose within the mind, shaped by past conditioning, comparison, and desire.

The moment itself was brief. It appeared and passed. It was impermanent. But the mind holds onto it, builds upon it, and turns it into a source of ongoing dissatisfaction. This is how even ordinary, harmless experiences can become a cause of suffering when the mind is untrained.

Consider another real-life scenario shared by a family member who is very dear to me. She once told me about an incident that caused her deep mental suffering.

She had invited relatives to her home for a special occasion. She took leave from work, spent hours cleaning the house, and prepared traditional food with great care and effort. Her intention was simple: to make everyone feel welcomed and valued.

The relatives came, spent time together, enjoyed the meal, and eventually left. On the surface, everything seemed fine. But something unexpected happened within her mind.

A thought arose: "They didn't appreciate me. They didn't even say thank you." From that single thought, the mind began to build a story: "I did so much for them, and they didn't value it. My efforts don't matter. Even my own family didn't support or acknowledge me."

As she identified with these thoughts, the story grew stronger. The mind created more layers: expectations, judgments, and emotional pain. She began to expect an apology, to replay the event repeatedly, and to feel hurt each time she thought about it.

Meanwhile, the relatives had moved on with their lives, likely unaware of the impact their silence had created. But within her, the experience continued to live on. The event itself had passed, but the thoughts and emotions remained, replaying again and again.

If we look closely, something becomes clear. The suffering did not come from the event alone, but from the meaning the mind attached to it, the expectation of appreciation, the identification with the thought "I was not valued," and the repeated mental replay of the situation.

The moment itself was brief. It happened and ended. It was impermanent. But the mind held onto it, turning it into a lasting source of pain. This is how even acts of kindness and love can become sources of suffering when expectations and identification take over.

I have witnessed this pattern countless times among many of my Indian friends and relatives. It is a mindset that I personally do not adhere to, and one that not everyone shares. There is often a deep concern about what others think, how one appears, what one wears, the car one drives, and the house one lives in.

A simple choice is rarely just a choice. It becomes a question of image, comparison, and approval. Thoughts arise like:

"What will people say? Will they judge me? Do I look successful enough?" From there, the mind begins to build stories, creating pressure, anxiety, and a subtle but persistent sense of dissatisfaction.

What is striking is that this concern often has little to do with reality. The "others" we worry about may not even be thinking about us at all, yet the mind creates an imagined audience and reacts to it. Over time, this constant need for approval and fear of judgment becomes deeply ingrained, shaping decisions, behaviour, and even self-worth. In this way, the mind traps itself, not because of actual events, but because of the meanings and identities it continuously creates and clings to.

These examples reveal a simple but profound truth: it is not the events themselves that trap us, but our identification with the thoughts and emotions they trigger. Whether it is a rude comment, a social comparison, a family expectation, or concern about how others perceive us, the pattern remains the same. The mind takes a single spark, a comment, a memory, or a comparison, and builds an entire narrative around it. Once we claim ownership over these mental events, we begin to suffer, often long after the original moment has passed.

The person who caused the offence, or the friend enjoying their vacation, may move through life fully present, unaffected by the story our mind has created. Meanwhile, we remain restless, replaying the events in our heads, trying to defend, protect, or correct the "self" that we imagine exists in these stories. This is how ordinary thoughts and emotions, harmless in themselves, become the source of so much internal struggle.

As we have seen, these thoughts and emotions do not arise from nowhere. They emerge naturally, shaped by conditions, our past experiences, habits, memories, and what we take in through our senses. They are part of the mind's ongoing process, appearing and fading according to circumstances beyond our immediate control. They persist because we cling to them, personalise them, or replay them, and suffering arises when we mistakenly identify with them.

One important realisation is this: the problem is not the thoughts, the emotions, or the feelings themselves. It is our relationship with them. Thoughts will arise. Emotions will come and go. This is their nature. But the moment we cling to them, identify with them, or resist them, they begin to take control of our inner world.

It is not the presence of thoughts that creates suffering, but the absence of awareness, the ability to observe them without identifying with them. When this relationship remains unconscious and unexamined, the mind becomes a place of struggle.

Understanding this is the first step. Once we see that thoughts and emotions are natural processes, not fixed truths about who we are, we begin to glimpse the possibility of observing the mind without being trapped inside it. This becomes a small but vital doorway toward clarity and peace.

Later in this book, I will share how I began to work with these thoughts and emotions, how I learned to observe the mind instead of being lost within it, and how Buddhist practices gradually guided me toward clarity, balance, and inner freedom. For now, the goal is simply to understand why these mental patterns arise and why they can feel so overwhelming.

10

Why There Is Suffering

If thoughts and emotions arise naturally, then a deeper question follows:

Why do they cause so much suffering?

If anger, fear, comparison, or sadness are simply natural processes of the mind, then why do they feel so heavy, so personal, and at times unbearable? Why does a single thought have the power to disturb our peace for hours, days, or even years?

The answer is subtle, yet profound. It lies in attachment and craving. From a Buddhist perspective, suffering, or dukkha, does not arise because life is inherently painful, but because of the mind's tendency to cling. We grasp at thoughts, emotions, experiences, and even identities as if they were permanent, as if we could make them stay. When they inevitably change, fade, or disappear, the mind reacts with resistance, frustration, and distress.

As the Buddha taught, *"From craving arises sorrow, from craving arises fear; for one who is free from craving, there is no sorrow. So how could there be fear?"* **(Dhammapada 216).**

Suffering, then, is not caused by the mere presence of thoughts and emotions, but by how we relate to them, how we cling to them, resist them, and build our identity around them. What we explored in the previous chapter, the identification with thoughts, is not just a habit. It is the very foundation of suffering.

This is what is meant by dukkha, a deep, underlying dissatisfaction that exists even when everything appears fine on the surface. It is not always loud or obvious. Sometimes it is quiet: a subtle restlessness, a feeling that something is missing, a sense that things are not quite as they should be.

The mind is constantly seeking. It seeks pleasure, approval, certainty, and control. It wants pleasant experiences to stay and unpleasant ones to disappear. But life does not follow these rules. Everything changes. Experiences come and go. People change. Situations shift.

And yet, the mind resists this reality.

It clings to what it likes.

It rejects what it dislikes.

It ignores what it does not understand.

This constant push and pull, this craving and resistance, is where suffering begins.

As you are reading this, I want to invite you into a simple reflection. Take a moment and answer honestly for yourself.

Consider these two situations:

Situation 1: Something pleasant happens in your life, a promotion at work, money flowing in, a luxury trip, a happy memory with loved ones, or a moment where everything feels just right. Almost immediately, the mind says, "I want this to stay. I don't want this to change."

For example, you receive good news about your finances, or

you are enjoying a beautiful holiday. In that moment, a subtle thought arises: "I wish this could last forever. I don't want to lose this feeling."

Situation 2: Now imagine something unpleasant happens, a breakup, a financial loss, a failure, or someone speaks harshly to you. Instantly, the mind reacts, "I don't want this. This shouldn't be happening. Make it stop."

For example, a relationship ends, or you face a sudden loss of money. The mind immediately resists: "Why did this happen to me? This is not fair. I can't accept this."

Now pause and ask yourself:

Which of these responses feels right? Which one do you believe will bring you peace and happiness?

Most people instinctively choose the first. That was my mindset as well. Holding onto what feels good seems natural, even desirable.

But when we look more deeply, something surprising becomes clear:

Both responses are rooted in the same problem.

In the first, there is craving, to hold on, to make something pleasant stay.

In the second, there is also craving, to push away, to resist, to make something unpleasant disappear.

In both cases, the mind is not at rest. It is making an effort, trying to control, trying to shape reality according to its preferences.

And wherever there is effort to control what cannot be controlled, there is tension.

Where there is tension, there is struggle.

And where there is struggle, there is no true peace.

This is the deeper truth:

Whether we cling to what we like or resist what we dislike, the mind remains trapped.

As the Buddha taught, "I*t is this craving which leads to renewed existence, accompanied by delight and lust, seeking delight here and there. That is, craving for sensual pleasures, craving for existence, and craving for non-existence.*" (**Samyutta Nikaya 56.11**)

At this point, a natural question arises:

If both clinging and resisting lead to suffering, then how should one deal with life?

How do we experience joy without trying to hold onto it?

How do we face pain without wanting to escape it?

How can the mind remain at peace when everything around it is constantly changing?

These are important questions. But before we rush to find answers, we must first understand the problem more deeply.

Because the mind is not just reacting to situations, it is conditioned to do so. This habit of craving and resistance is not something we consciously choose each time. It is deeply ingrained. It has been built over the years through experiences, beliefs, fears, and desires.

This is why suffering feels so automatic. A situation happens, and almost instantly, the mind moves, grasping, rejecting, judging, comparing, without any awareness of what it is doing.

What appears to be a simple reaction is, in reality, a deeply rooted pattern.

And until this pattern is clearly seen and understood, any attempt to fix the mind or force peace will only create more struggle.

So for now, the goal is not to change anything.

The goal is to see clearly, to understand how suffering is created within the mind itself. Only from that clarity can something real begin to shift.

I did not understand any of this at first. For a long time, I was caught in the same patterns, holding on to what felt good, resisting what felt painful, and constantly trying to control what was never in my control. It felt natural, even justified, but it also left me restless and unsettled.

It was only later, through Buddhist wisdom and my own direct experience, that I began to see this clearly. What I once believed was normal was actually the very source of my inner struggle.

I will share more about how this understanding unfolded in my life, and how I began to work with these patterns, in the chapters ahead. For now, it is enough to recognise that this cycle of craving and resistance is something many of us live with, often without ever questioning it.

The path out of suffering does not begin with escape. It begins with understanding. Until you see how it arises, you cannot truly find freedom from it.

11

Attachment, Craving, and the Illusion of Control

In the previous chapter, we explored the root of suffering and how craving and resistance trap the mind. We saw that whether we cling to what we like or push away what we dislike, tension and struggle inevitably arise.

Now, let us go deeper. The mind does not only cling to fleeting thoughts, emotions, or pleasant experiences. It extends attachment to people, possessions, beliefs, and even the identities we create for ourselves. It is this craving that creates the illusion of control, the belief that we can hold on to happiness, prevent loss, or dictate how life unfolds. And it is this illusion that keeps the mind restless, caught in cycles of dissatisfaction.

Attachment to People

We naturally form bonds with others, but attachment arises when we try to control how they behave or expect them to meet our desires. A spouse, friend, or child may act in a way that disappoints us, or simply change over time. Instantly, the mind reacts, and worry, fear, anger, or sadness arise.

I remember a time when a close friend started taking longer to respond to my messages. Each unread notification made my chest tighten, and my mind began spinning: Have I done something wrong? Did I say something to upset him? Am I losing his friendship? I replayed every conversation, every joke, every word, searching for a mistake that didn't exist. In reality, my friend was simply busy, wrapped up in his own life, unaware of the storm in my mind.

On another occasion, a close relative and I had a minor disagreement during a vacation. Afterwards, he didn't call for months, and I didn't reach out either. I imagined all sorts of scenarios: Is he angry with me? Has he stopped caring? Have I ruined our relationship? My mind built an entire narrative from a single event. The truth was far simpler, yet my attachment, the need for reassurance and control over how others felt, turned a brief misunderstanding into weeks of unnecessary tension.

Looking back, I see clearly now that it was not the silence, the disagreement, or the delay that caused the suffering. It was my own attachment, my insistence that the world conform to my expectations, that kept me trapped.

Consider a spouse or partner you've known for years. Over time, people change, interests shift, priorities evolve, and moods fluctuate, but the mind clings to an idea of who they should be. I remember feeling frustrated when my wife started spending more time on work projects, leaving less time for our usual conversations. My mind reacted: Why is this happening? Doesn't she care about me? Are we drifting apart? I tried to control the situation by suggesting more time together and checking in constantly, but the more I tried, the more tense things became.

It was only later that I realised I was not frustrated with her, but with the illusion of control I had created. Love cannot be owned or managed. It is given freely. Marriage is not ownership; it is walking together. The moment I loosened my grip and allowed my wife to be herself, finding joy in her happiness and what she does, the tension eased. Even if our routines did not look exactly as I had imagined, a quiet sense of peace returned, and our relationship grew stronger.

Or consider a parent who worries constantly about a child's future. The child is growing, learning, and making their own choices, yet the parent clings to control: I must protect them. I must guide them. I cannot let anything go wrong. Even natural care can turn into anxiety, creating tension for both parent and child, and leaving little space for ease.

What makes this suffering so subtle is that it often appears as love, care, or responsibility. We convince ourselves that our worry and expectations are necessary. Yet the deeper truth is simple. The more we try to hold on to people or shape them according to our desires, the more tension we create. Attachment turns a natural relationship into a source of inner struggle.

As the Buddha taught, *"What is impermanent, suffering, and subject to change, is it fit to be regarded as: 'This is mine, this I am, this is my self?'"* **(Samyutta Nikaya 22.59).** This is where attachment begins, when we turn relationships into something we believe we own or control.

It is important to understand what this truly means. Letting go of attachment to people does not mean leaving them or ignoring them. It means releasing the need to control how they think, feel, or behave. It means allowing them to be themselves, while offering love freely, without expectation. True connection grows not from control, but from acceptance.

Attachment to Possessions

We often tie our sense of security and self-worth to material things. Money, property, cars, or even a high-paying job can become extensions of our identity. A promotion, a raise, or a new home may bring joy, but when we cling to these things as if they define us, suffering follows.

Imagine finally getting a job you have been striving for. At first, it feels exciting. But soon the mind begins to worry: What if I lose it? What if someone else is better than me? What if I fail? In the same way, buying a car or moving into a new home may bring satisfaction, but fear of loss or damage soon follows.

Even simple possessions like phones or everyday items can create subtle anxiety when they are threatened. The mind clings, judges, and resists their impermanent nature.

It is important to distinguish between what we need and what we crave. Having shelter, money, and basic comfort supports life. But craving more, or identifying ourselves with possessions, turns these into sources of tension. The more we try to hold on to them, the more restless the mind becomes.

As the Buddha said, *"Riches ruin the foolish, but not those who seek the other shore. By craving for riches, the foolish ruin themselves as if they were their own enemy"* **(Dhammapada 355).**

Attachment to possessions creates suffering, not because the objects are bad, but because the mind tries to make them permanent and secure. The moment we see their changing nature and loosen our grip, tension begins to ease.

Attachment to Beliefs

Just as the mind clings to people and possessions, it also clings to ideas and beliefs. These may be religious, spiritual, or personal. At first, beliefs guide us. But when the mind insists that they must be true and others must agree, suffering arises.

This can be seen everywhere. People argue over beliefs, and even within the same group, there are divisions and conflicts. A simple disagreement can quickly turn into tension. The mind feels threatened and reacts: They are wrong. I am right.

This suffering does not come from the other person being wrong. It comes from attachment to one's own view.

Attachment to beliefs creates both pride and fear. Pride arises when we feel certain we are right, and fear arises when those beliefs are challenged. This is another form of craving, the need to be right and to feel secure.

The Buddha warned about this. In the **Kalama Sutta**, he advised, *"Do not go upon what has been acquired by repeated hearing, nor upon tradition, nor upon rumor, nor upon what is in a scripture... When you know for yourselves that these things are unwholesome... then you should abandon them"* (**Anguttara Nikaya 3.65**).

Letting go of attachment to beliefs does not mean abandoning values. It means remaining open, willing to question, and not forcing reality to fit our ideas. When the mind relaxes its grip, there is less defensiveness and more clarity.

The Illusion of Control

At the heart of all attachment is the belief that we can control life, that we can hold on to happiness and avoid pain. But life does not follow our preferences. People change. Possessions fade. Situations shift. Beliefs are challenged.

Yet the mind resists this truth and tries to impose its will.

Whether it is a person, a possession, or a belief, the pattern is the same. The mind tries to hold on or push away. Tension builds, and peace remains out of reach.

This is the cycle described in Buddhist teaching as samsara, the repeated pattern of craving and dissatisfaction. As the Buddha taught, *"It is this craving which leads to renewed existence, accompanied by delight and lust, seeking delight here and there. That is, craving for sensual pleasures, craving for existence, and craving for non-existence"* **(Samyutta Nikaya 56.11).**

Every attempt to control, hold, or resist life strengthens this illusion and keeps the mind trapped.

12

The Trap of Escaping the Problem

Before we move forward, it is important to notice one more pattern: how we try to escape the problem without truly understanding it. Many people attempt to move away from the unrest of the mind without seeing its nature.

Most of us feel it at some point, a quiet unease, a restlessness, a sense that something is not quite right within. But instead of turning toward it, we try to move away. We look for ways to escape what we feel.

When the mind feels restless, anxious, or unsettled, it immediately seeks relief. This too is a form of craving, the desire to get away from discomfort. This urge to avoid, suppress, or escape what we feel is part of the same cycle that keeps the mind trapped.

Some chase success, believing achievement will finally bring peace. Others turn to possessions, thinking more will create security. Many fill their time with constant activity, entertainment, or social media to avoid sitting with their own thoughts.

Some turn to alcohol, drugs, or other substances to numb

what they feel. For a moment, it may bring relief or distraction. But over time, it often deepens the problem, creating dependency and making the mind even more sensitive and unsettled.

Some turn deeply toward religion or belief systems, moving from one teaching to another, repeatedly seeking certainty or answers in texts, teachers, or practices. I did this too, constantly shifting, thinking the next insight would finally settle the mind. But the unrest remained, because the root was never addressed.

Others begin to avoid. They steer clear of people, places, or situations that trigger anxiety or discomfort. A person may stop visiting certain locations, avoid conversations, or withdraw from relationships, not because the world is dangerous, but because the mind feels overwhelmed. I have done all of this, and it only added to the weight.

At first, these strategies bring relief. But slowly, the world becomes smaller, and the mind becomes more sensitive and reactive. What is avoided does not disappear. It grows stronger.

For a moment, the mind may feel occupied or distracted. But beneath it all, the same unrest remains, waiting quietly. The problem is not removed. It is only covered. The next time fear, anxiety, or inner conflict arises, it often feels stronger, because avoiding it has made it more insistent and harder to face.

This is how the cycle deepens. Whether through success, distraction, belief, or avoidance, the mind still operates from the same place, craving relief and trying to control experience. For a moment, it may seem effective. But beneath the surface, nothing has truly changed.

In fact, the more we try to escape, the harder it becomes to face the mind. When fear, anxiety, or inner conflict arises again, it often feels stronger. What we resist does not weaken. It persists.

This is the trap. We believe we are solving the problem, but we are only moving away from it.

Real change does not begin with escape. It begins with understanding.

To understand the problem deeply, we must turn toward the mind itself, how it works, why it reacts the way it does, and why it keeps repeating these patterns. Only then can something real begin to shift.

Practice Pause: Notice Your Mind

Before moving forward, take a brief moment to pause and simply notice your own mind. You do not need to change anything or fix a single thought. Just watch.

Sit quietly for a minute and let your body relax.

Allow your thoughts to arise and pass, like clouds drifting across the sky.

Notice any cravings, distractions, or subtle urges to avoid discomfort.

Observe how your mind reacts, without judgment or trying to control it.

This small pause may feel insignificant, but it is the first step toward seeing your patterns clearly. Awareness itself, simply noticing the mind at work, is where real change begins. Even one quiet moment of observing without judgment begins to uncover the peace that has always been there.

Part 1 Summary: Understanding the Problem

Thoughts and emotions do not arise randomly. They arise when certain conditions are present, such as past experiences, habits, memories, and what we take in through our senses. A thought appears, an emotion follows, and the mind begins to react.

This is where the struggle begins. The mind identifies with these thoughts and emotions, treating them as personal and real. It clings to what it likes and resists what it dislikes, creating tension, conflict, and inner unrest.

This unrest is shaped by attachment, craving, and the desire to control experiences, people, and beliefs. The mind tries to hold on to what feels good and push away what feels uncomfortable, but in doing so, it becomes trapped in repeating cycles of tension.

When discomfort arises, the mind moves away from it. It seeks relief through achievement, possessions, distraction, belief systems, or avoidance. For a moment, this may seem to help. But the problem is not resolved. It remains beneath the surface.

Over time, the same thoughts and emotions return, often with greater intensity. The cycle continues, not because something is wrong with us, but because the mind is operating in patterns that have not yet been clearly seen.

PART 2: UNDERSTANDING THE PROBLEM

How the mind creates suffering and keeps the cycle going.

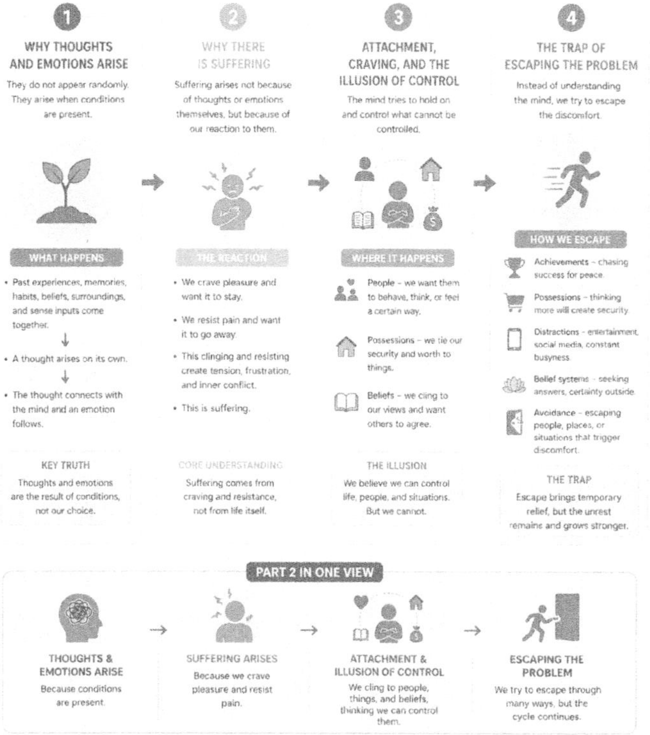

III

Understanding the Mind

These chapters explore the mind itself, how it works, why it reacts, and why peace can feel elusive. We examine its survival-focused nature, how thoughts and cravings trap us, and why patterns of unrest continue. This section prepares you to see clearly, so that when we move to practice, real change and peace become possible.

13

What Is the Mind, and Where Is It?

Pause for a moment and ask yourself a simple question: What is the mind? Where is it?

We use this word every day. We say, "My mind is busy," "My mind is tired," or "I can't stop thinking." But if we look closely, it becomes difficult to define.

Where is the mind? Can you point to it? Is it in the brain, in the body, or somewhere else entirely?

If you look closely, it becomes difficult to locate the mind in any one place. It is not something fixed that you can point to. It appears through thoughts, emotions, and awareness, constantly changing and moving.

So where is the mind?

It is not something we can point to like an object. The mind appears wherever experience is happening, in thoughts, in emotions, and in awareness. It is something we experience, not something we can hold or find.

What we call "mind" appears as thoughts, emotions, memories, and reactions. A thought arises, then another, then another. Emotions come and go, sometimes quickly, sometimes lingering. Memories appear without invitation. Plans for the future form on their own. This constant movement is what most of us call the mind.

I remember times when my mind felt completely out of control. Thoughts would come one after another, without any effort from me. Even when I wanted silence, the mind kept going. It made me realise something important. I was not creating every thought. They were simply appearing.

Think about when you are stuck in traffic, late for an appointment. Instantly, thoughts arise: Why is everyone driving so slowly? I'll be late. What if they get angry at me? Alongside these thoughts, frustration and tension build in your body. Your chest tightens, and your hands grip the steering wheel. Yet if you pause for a moment, you may notice that these thoughts and feelings arose on their own. You did not consciously summon them.

Or consider waking up to a critical email from your boss. Your mind races: Did I make a mistake? How will I explain this? What if I lose my job? Again, the thoughts arrive uninvited, accompanied by anxiety, restlessness, and even discomfort in the body. If we follow them blindly, they can spiral for hours or days. But if we simply observe them, the intensity can begin to soften.

Or notice what happens when a friend cancels plans unexpectedly. The mind may immediately imagine scenarios: Do they not like me anymore? Did I say something wrong? Am I being ignored? Emotions arise: hurt, anger, disappointment. Yet these are processes happening in awareness, not commands we must obey.

But is that all the mind is?

If you observe carefully, something interesting becomes

clear. You are able to notice your thoughts. You can say, "I am thinking." You can also notice your emotions: "I feel anxious," "I feel happy," "I feel angry."

If thoughts and emotions can be observed, then a deeper question arises:

Who is the one observing them?

This is where a subtle but powerful shift begins. The mind is not just the thoughts and emotions themselves. It also includes the awareness that knows them. There is a difference between a thought arising and the awareness that notices it. There is a difference between anger arising and the awareness that sees it.

From a Buddhist perspective, this distinction is essential. The Buddha taught that what we take to be "self" is not a fixed entity, but a collection of changing processes. In the Anatta (non-self) teaching, he points out that thoughts, feelings, and perceptions are not truly "mine" or "me," because they arise and pass away on their own.

As it is said in the teachings, *"This is not mine, this I am not, this is not my self"* (**Samyutta Nikaya 22.59**).

This does not mean that we deny our experience. Thoughts and emotions still arise. But it invites us to see them differently, not as who we are, but as processes happening within awareness.

To understand this, you don't need to believe anything. You can observe it directly.

Right now, as you are reading, notice your next thought.

Did you choose it, or did it simply appear?

Notice a feeling in your body.

Did you create it, or did it arise on its own?

And yet, something is aware of both.

This simple observation is the beginning of mindfulness, not a technique to control the mind, but a way of seeing clearly. Mindfulness is the ability to observe thoughts, emotions, and sensations as they arise, without immediately identifying with them or reacting to them.

The Buddha described this in the practice of awareness, where one observes the body, feelings, and mind as they are, simply noticing what is present, without clinging or resisting (**Satipatthana Sutta, MN 10**).

At first, this may seem subtle. The habit of identifying with the mind is strong. The moment a thought arises, we follow it. The moment an emotion appears, we become it. This is how we have lived for most of our lives.

But with even a small shift in awareness, something begins to change.

Instead of being lost in thought, you begin to see the thought.

Instead of being overwhelmed by emotion, you begin to notice the emotion.

I noticed this in small moments. A thought would arise, and instead of reacting immediately, there was a brief pause. In that pause, I could see the thought rather than become it. It was simple, but it changed everything.

Imagine receiving criticism from a colleague at work. Normally, your mind might spiral into defensiveness or resentment. But with observation, you see: this is just a thought arising. This is just a feeling arising. The situation is the same, but your reaction can be calmer and less automatic.

Or consider receiving unexpected praise for something you did. Excitement and pride arise, pleasant yet fleeting. Observing them allows you to enjoy them without clinging or expecting them to last forever.

In that small space between awareness and the mind, there is a sense of ease, even if brief.

This is important to understand. The goal is not to stop thinking. The mind will continue to produce thoughts. That is its nature. The goal is simply to see clearly, to recognise that thoughts and emotions are not who we are.

As this understanding deepens, the grip of the mind begins to loosen. Thoughts may still arise, but they no longer carry the same weight. Emotions may still come, but they pass more freely.

You begin to experience something new, not something created, but something revealed.

The mind is not a fixed thing, and it is not located in one place. It is a flow of thoughts, emotions, and awareness, appearing wherever experience is happening.

And within that, something quiet is always present. A simple awareness that has always been there, beneath the noise of the mind.

The mind is not something to find. It is something to see clearly.

14

The Function of the Mind: Survival, Not Peace

The mind is a remarkable tool. It notices, plans, evaluates, and reacts.

Do you know the function of the mind? Many, like me before, might confidently say, "The mind is designed for peace; it helps me relax, focus, or feel calm." But the truth is surprising: the mind is not naturally oriented toward peace. Its primary function is survival.

From the earliest moments of life, the mind has been tuned to detect threats, avoid danger, and secure resources. This survival-oriented programming explains why the mind is often restless, anxious, and reactive.

Even ancient humans were built this way. Imagine our ancestors living in caves, always watching for predators, listening for sudden noises, and staying alert for anything that could threaten their lives. Their minds were finely tuned for survival, designed to notice danger before it could strike. Today, that same mind, made to keep us alive, often makes mistakes, seeing threats where there are none, imagining dangers that are not real, and reacting to thoughts and situations as if they were a matter of life and death.

The mind wants to protect you. That is its role. But in trying to protect you from every possible danger, it can become overactive and controlling. Instead of keeping you safe, it can begin to trap you. What once served as protection slowly turns into a prison, where every thought is treated as a threat, and every feeling needs to be managed or escaped.

Think about your daily life. A colleague sends a short, sharp email. Immediately, the mind jumps to conclusions: Are they upset with me? Did I make a mistake? Could this hurt my job? Your heart beats faster, your chest feels tight, and tension spreads through your body.

Or imagine driving home in heavy traffic. Every honk, every sudden stop sets your mind on alert. You keep thinking: Am I safe? Will I get home on time? What if something goes wrong?

Even positive events can trigger survival reactions. You get a promotion at work. Your mind immediately begins calculating: How can I maintain this status? Will expectations increase? What if I fail? Excitement and joy are mixed with subtle anxiety. The mind is not interested in peace; it is wired to anticipate, to protect, and to prepare for what comes next.

Buddhist teachings recognise this deeply. The Buddha explained that the mind is conditioned by ignorance and craving, always seeking what is favorable and avoiding what is unfavorable. In the **Samyutta Nikaya (SN 12.2),** he describes how, with ignorance as a condition, reactions arise, and from these, craving and clinging follow. This is not a moral failing; it is the mind doing exactly what it is designed to do. Awareness of this tendency is crucial because most of us mistake this restless activity for a problem we must fix, rather than a natural function.

Consider the parent awake at night, listening for any sign of danger while the child sleeps. The heightened alertness, the worry, and the constant scanning of possibilities are all rooted in the mind's survival instinct. Or the student preparing for exams, stressed over every potential mistake, imagining worst-case scenarios. The mind is simply doing its job, alert, anticipating threats, and trying to prevent harm.

Now consider someone who has just bought their dream house. After years of hard work, they finally move in, decorate it beautifully, and fill it with expensive furniture. It should be a time of peace and joy. But soon, the mind shifts into survival mode: What if someone breaks in? What if something gets damaged? What if I lose all this? Even when they go away for a night, they keep checking their phone, thinking about security cameras, worrying about every possible risk. What was meant to bring comfort slowly becomes a source of tension.

Or think about someone who buys an expensive car they had always dreamed of. At first, there is excitement and pride. But soon, the mind becomes alert and protective: Did someone scratch it? Where should I park so it is safe? What if it gets stolen? Every small mark becomes a concern. Instead of enjoying the car, they find themselves constantly checking, worrying, and guarding it.

Or consider someone who invests a large amount of money. Even if the investment is doing well, the mind does not rest. It keeps checking: What if the market crashes? Should I sell? What if I lose everything? The numbers may go up, but the mind keeps scanning for danger, unable to relax.

Or think about a person posting something on social media. After posting, the mind keeps returning: How many likes did

I get? Why didn't that person respond? Did people like it or judge me? A simple act turns into continuous checking and subtle anxiety.

Even in relationships, the survival mind shows its influence. When a loved one disagrees with us, we feel attacked, rejected, or unsafe. We interpret the disagreement as a threat to our identity or social standing. The mind reacts automatically: defend, argue, or withdraw. This pattern is not inherently wrong; it is survival in action, but it creates tension and conflict when we mistake it for the whole of reality.

In all these situations, nothing is immediately wrong. There is no real danger in that moment. And yet, the mind behaves as if something must be protected, controlled, or secured. It keeps scanning, predicting, and preparing. This is not a flaw; it is exactly what the mind was built to do.

As the Buddha observed, *"The mind is restless, difficult to guard, and hard to control; the wise person straightens it as a fletcher straightens an arrow"* (**Dhammapada 33**).

The mind's survival function also explains why we struggle with change. Life is impermanent: people, possessions, opportunities, and even our own bodies shift constantly. The survival mind perceives change as potential danger. This is why uncertainty feels uncomfortable, why loss provokes anxiety, and why the unknown triggers stress. The mind's response is automatic, even when there is no real threat; our imagination magnifies possible harm.

A simple illustration: you are walking down the street and hear a loud bang. Instantly, adrenaline surges, your muscles tense, and your heart races. Even if you quickly realise it was nothing, the mind cannot help but react. This same mechanism underlies much of our daily worry, planning, and anticipation, even when danger is minimal or imagined.

The survival mind is useful; it keeps us alive, attentive, and responsive. But it is not oriented toward inner peace. Peace is not its goal.

That is why meditation, mindfulness, and awareness practices are so important. They do not try to shut down the mind or stop thoughts. Instead, they help us recognise the mind's survival patterns, observe them, and create a space in which peace can emerge naturally.

As the Buddha taught in the **Satipatthana Sutta (MN 10)**, we practice awareness of the body, feelings, mind, and phenomena to see clearly what arises. By observing our natural survival reactions without automatically identifying with them, we begin to loosen the grip of restlessness. We see that anxious thoughts, fears, and reactive emotions are natural, but they are not the whole of who we are.

Understanding the mind's function is not a solution in itself, but it is a necessary foundation. When we see that much of our suffering arises from the mind's survival programming, not from the world or other people, we can begin to respond differently. We start to notice the patterns, recognise their purpose, and slowly allow a different kind of response, one guided by awareness rather than automatic reaction.

Peace is not something the mind creates; it is something that becomes visible when we understand the mind. By seeing the mind's survival focus clearly, we gain perspective. We are no longer at its mercy. The more we observe, the more we realise that what feels urgent, threatening, or critical is often a survival instinct reacting to imagined danger. And in that space of understanding, we begin to glimpse the possibility of ease, clarity, and true rest.

The Mind Is Not the Enemy

Many people believe the mind is the problem. I believed this for years.

When thoughts become overwhelming, when anxiety rises, and when overthinking takes over, it can feel like the mind is working against us. It may even feel like something inside is broken. But what if the mind is not the enemy?

The mind is not the enemy. It is simply doing what it was designed to do, thinking, analysing, and trying to protect you. Thoughts will always arise, just as breathing happens naturally.

Think of the mind like a smoke alarm. Its job is to detect danger and alert you. But sometimes, it goes off even when there is no real fire, just a bit of smoke. The alarm is not the problem. It is doing its job. The difficulty comes when we panic and assume there is danger every time it sounds.

Or think of the mind like a GPS. Its job is to guide you and keep you on track. But sometimes, even when you are already on the right route, it keeps saying, "Recalculating... recalculating..."

At times, it suggests a different route just to save a minute or two, or because it thinks the road might be smoother. Imagine you are driving home from work. You already know the way, but the GPS keeps changing directions, asking you to turn here or there. If you follow every change, you may feel confused or stressed, even though you were already on a perfectly fine path.

The GPS is not broken. It is trying to help. But reacting to every update makes the journey harder.

In the same way, the mind keeps analysing, correcting, and predicting. It is not your enemy. It is simply trying to guide and protect you, even when there is no real danger.

The problem is not the thoughts themselves, but how we relate to them. When we believe every thought, react to it, or try to control it, we create unnecessary suffering.

You do not need to fight the mind. You only need to understand it.

15

Why Peace Feels Out of Reach

Do you ever wonder why, despite all your efforts, peace seems just out of reach? People acquire properties, achieve goals, and gather possessions, yet peace remains distant. Many, like me before, believe that peace is something to achieve, something to create through effort, discipline, control, or escape. But the truth is simple and surprising: peace is not something to make or create. It has always been with us. Peace exists in the quiet space between thoughts, emotions, and sensations. It is not created; it is uncovered.

Most people keep chasing peace, trying to create it, because they do not realise it is already there. And so peace always seems just out of reach. The mind is restless and often works against what we tell it. You cannot command it to be calm; it has its own nature.

Try this: tell yourself, "Don't think about anything for a moment." Notice how quickly thoughts begin to appear on their own.

The same happens in everyday life. You tell yourself, "Don't worry about work," and immediately your mind starts replaying all the tasks, deadlines, and what-ifs. You try to stop feeling jealous when a friend succeeds, but your mind keeps comparing, calculating, and imagining scenarios. You say, "Don't get angry," yet every small annoyance suddenly feels magnified, and tension spreads through your body. You try to sleep, thinking, "Don't think about tomorrow—I want to rest," and suddenly your mind is racing through the day's to-do list and worries.

The more we try to control the mind, the more it resists. It spins, imagines, anticipates, and obsesses, not because we are failing, but because that is its nature. Understanding this is the first step toward uncovering the peace that has always been with us.

Have you ever noticed that when you were born and began to grow, your mind was quiet and fully present? Peace was always there. There was no overthinking, no craving, and no attachment to anyone or anything. Everything was experienced simply and directly. But as we grow, the mind begins to fill with chatter, with endless thoughts, worries, and desires. That quiet space where peace naturally exists becomes crowded and buried under mental noise.

Later in life, when people reach their final phase, many return to a simple calm. Their cravings have faded, attachments have loosened, and the constant need to fix or control things is gone. Peace emerges naturally and effortlessly.

Peace is always there. It exists in the space between thoughts. The more the mind fills with thinking, the less space remains for peace. When thoughts quiet down, even slightly, that space opens, and peace can be felt. It is subtle and cannot be forced. It is not achieved through effort, but discovered, like noticing a stillness that has always been present.

Think of it like your daily commute. Imagine driving from work to home during peak hours. The road is crowded, traffic moves slowly, some drivers are aggressive, and small delays or incidents create stress. Every turn, every honk, every stoplight demands your attention, and tension rises.

Now imagine taking the same route late at night, when traffic is light, the streets are quiet, and the drive is smooth. The road is the same, the vehicle is the same, and you are the same driver, but the experience is completely different.

In the busy hours, the calmness of the road is buried beneath noise, chaos, and constant demands. At night, that same calm is visible, accessible, and effortless. Peace is always there, just like the smooth road at night, but in daily life, it is often hidden beneath the clutter of thoughts, worries, and distractions.

Peace is always here, but mental clutter, distraction, and overthinking cover it up. The mind rarely allows us to notice this peace. As we explored in Chapter 13, the mind is designed for survival, not calm. It constantly reacts, evaluates, and anticipates danger, even in ordinary, safe situations. Add to that the attachments and cravings we discussed in Chapter 11—our desire to control people, possessions, and beliefs—and you have a mind that is endlessly busy. The result is a constant stream of mental chatter: worries, judgments, what-ifs, and regrets.

This is why peace seems so elusive. We are trying to grasp it with a mind that is designed to scan for danger, react to cravings, and hold on to attachments. But peace is not something to capture. It is the natural state that becomes visible when the constant clatter of thoughts and emotions is noticed and allowed to settle. It exists in the gaps, the pauses, the silent spaces we often overlook.

The Buddha recognised this clearly. He said: "*The mind is restless, fickle, hard to guard, and difficult to control, wandering wherever it likes, like a monkey that leaps from one branch to another*" (**Anguttara Nikaya 7.66**). This is exactly how our minds operate today: swinging from thought to thought, from fear to desire, from craving to regret. It is not evil or wrong—it is simply the mind functioning for survival. When we fail to notice the silent space behind the mind's activity, we mistakenly believe that peace is missing, when in fact it has been present all along.

Consider a moment when your mind quiets naturally—a deep breath, a pause in conversation, watching the sunset, or listening to gentle music. For an instant, the mental chatter fades, and peace is felt, even if briefly. This is not something created; it is uncovered.

With awareness and gentle observation, these moments expand. The gaps between thoughts lengthen, reactions soften, and the mind's habitual alertness eases.

Peace is already here. The mind does not need to create it, control it, or force it. What is needed is understanding, observation, and patience. Recognising the mind's survival instinct, its cravings, and its constant activity allows us to step back and see clearly.

The chaos of thought and emotion is just activity; it is not the essence of who we are. And in that recognition, the ever-present space of peace becomes visible, available, and alive.

16

Patterns of the Mind

Have you ever noticed that your mind doesn't just think? It repeats.

The same thoughts come again and again. The same worries return. The same questions replay, even when there are no answers left to find. It feels as if the mind is stuck in a loop, going over the same ground, unable to move on.

This is not random. The mind operates in patterns.

Some patterns are easy to recognise. The mind may keep replaying the past, going over the same events again and again. This is often called rumination. At other times, it jumps into the future, creating endless "what-if" scenarios. Worry loops that never seem to end. In some cases, the mind becomes obsessive, needing certainty, repeating thoughts, or checking again and again. This is similar to what many experience as OCD (Obsessive-Compulsive Disorder), sometimes visible in actions, and sometimes only happening silently in the mind.

I have experienced many of these patterns at different times in my life. But the most difficult was a form of obsessive thinking that happened only in the mind. There were no visible actions, just constant repetition of thoughts, questions, and the need for certainty. I didn't even know what to call it at the time. Honestly, it felt like it was taking over my life.

A single thought would arise. The moment I engaged with it, it would grow into a story. Then into a series of episodes, playing again and again in my mind. There were no outward signs, nothing anyone else could see. But inside, it was relentless.

The same sentence would repeat once, then again, then again. Four times, six times, eight times. Because I felt I wouldn't get relief unless I kept repeating it. Over time, this became a pattern of thought. Automatic, repetitive, and hard to break. It was like being trapped in a loop I couldn't escape. The more I tried to control it, suppress it, or fight it, the stronger it became.

It was exhausting, unsettling, and at times overwhelming. Like being stuck inside my own mind with no pause, no silence, and no escape.

These patterns can be subtle or intense. Sometimes they appear outwardly, and other times they exist only within the mind, quietly repeating.

As we explored in Chapter 14, the mind is designed for survival, not peace. It scans for problems, tries to solve them, and holds on to anything that feels unfinished or uncertain. But sometimes, instead of solving, it gets caught in repetition.

In some cases, this pattern becomes even more intense, like what many experience as OCD. Sometimes with visible actions, and sometimes only within the mind. In both, there is a deep urge to repeat, driven by the hope of relief. The person often knows it doesn't make sense. They may even feel embarrassed or frustrated, especially when others are watching. They don't want to repeat, but at the same time, they feel they have no choice. Because until they do, the mind does not settle.

This is the painful reality of such patterns. The mind learns that repetition brings a brief sense of relief, and so it keeps returning to it. Over time, this becomes a cycle. Almost like an addiction. The more it is followed, the stronger it grows, draining mental energy and even affecting the body.

It can feel like being trapped in your own mind, fighting something invisible, something others may never fully see. And at its worst, it truly feels like a kind of living hell. Not because something is wrong with you, but because the mind has fallen into a pattern it does not yet understand.

There were times when my mind would go back many years into the past, replaying situations again and again. I would question what happened, why it happened, why someone said or did something, and what I could have done differently. I would even ask people around me, including my wife, to help me find answers, hoping that clarity would finally bring relief.

But the relief never lasted. The surprising part was that most of those people didn't even remember the events in detail. How could they? It had been years. Yet my mind held onto it as if it had just happened yesterday.

The mind kept returning to the same story, the same question, the same doubt.

This is what we call rumination. Repeating the past, trying to fix what cannot be changed.

What made it even more intense was how these patterns attached themselves to daily life. They would arise at the same moments, almost like triggers. When I stepped into the shower and the water hit. When I took the first bite of a meal. When I started the car. When I lie down to sleep. Or even the moment I woke up. It felt like the mind was waiting for these moments to restart the same loop, again and again, every single day.

When rumination and obsessive thinking came together, it felt like they took everything from me. It was as if my mind had become a director, creating the same movie over and over again. A movie that would never be released, never finished, never resolved.

At other times, the mind moved into worry loops. It would jump into the future, imagining scenarios that had not happened and might never happen. What if something goes wrong? What if I fail? What if things don't work out?

One thought would lead to another, then another, forming a chain that felt endless.

There were also patterns that felt like compulsion. Not always physical, but mental. The constant need to check, to be certain, to confirm, to get the "right" answer, again and again. Even when nothing was wrong, the mind kept searching, probing, repeating, as if something essential was missing. Every pattern, every loop felt hopeless, and I would tell myself, "This is the last time I will look for an answer to find relief."

And the hardest part was this. There was never a final answer.

This is similar to what many experience as obsessive patterns. Sometimes visible in actions, and sometimes only happening silently in the mind.

What makes these patterns so powerful is that they feel urgent, even essential. Each thought carries a sense of importance:

"You must figure this out."

"This matters."

"Don't ignore this."

"I must find the answer."

And so we follow, believing relief or clarity is just one more repetition away.

But if we pause and observe carefully, something becomes clear. The pattern is repeating, not resolving. The mind is not uncovering answers. It is circling, looping endlessly, creating the illusion of progress while trapping us in mental motion.

This can be exhausting. It drains energy, clouds judgment, and strains relationships. It pulls us away from the present moment, leaving life moving forward without us. The past replays, the future is feared, and the present, the only place we actually live, is taken over by the mind's loops.

Why does this happen?

Because the survival mind does not like uncertainty. It tries to close every loop, answer every question, and eliminate every possible risk. When it cannot, it keeps trying, again and again.

But some questions do not have answers.

Some situations cannot be undone.

Some uncertainty cannot be removed.

And yet, the mind continues.

The problem is not that thoughts arise. That is natural. The problem is that we believe every thought must be followed, solved, or completed.

As the Buddha pointed out, the mind tends to wander and cling, moving from one object to another, driven by craving and aversion. This wandering, repetitive nature is not a personal failure. It is simply how the untrained mind behaves.

"All that we are is the result of what we have thought. It is founded on our thoughts, it is made up of our thoughts" (**Dhammapada 1**).

When we do not see this clearly, we get trapped inside these patterns. The Buddha also emphasised the restless nature of the mind: *"The mind is restless, fickle, hard to guard, and difficult to control, wandering wherever it likes"* (**Anguttara Nikaya** 7.66).

Practice Pause: Watch the Mind at Work

Take a brief moment to pause and watch the mind at work.

You do not need to stop any thought or create calm. Just observe.

Sit quietly for a minute and let your body relax.

Notice how thoughts arise on their own.

Notice how one thought leads to another.

Notice whether the mind returns to the past, jumps into the future, or searches for certainty.

Watch the movement without trying to interfere.

This small pause reveals something important. The mind is always active. It is thinking, reacting, repeating, and searching. Seeing this clearly is the beginning of understanding the mind.

Part 3 Summary: Understanding the Mind

The mind is not a fixed thing. It is a flow of thoughts, emotions, and awareness, always changing.

It does not exist in one place. It appears through experience.

Its primary function is survival, not peace. It scans for danger, reacts to uncertainty, and tries to protect and control.

Because of this, peace often feels distant. The more we try to control the mind, the more restless it becomes.

The mind also moves in patterns. It repeats the past, worries about the future, and seeks certainty through constant thinking, sometimes becoming obsessive or repetitive.

These patterns do not bring resolution. They keep the mind in motion.

Understanding this is essential. The mind is not broken. It

is doing what it was designed to do.

But without awareness, it creates ongoing unrest.

IV

The Path to Calm and Clarity

This section marks the shift from understanding to practice, where insight begins to take shape in real life. Drawing on Buddhist wisdom and practices, along with my direct experience of understanding the problem and the mind, we learn to observe thoughts without attachment, embrace impermanence, and recognise the true nature of the mind. Through mindfulness and reflection, we discover how to ease suffering, release craving, and become the calm, aware witness of the mind in everyday life.

17

Don't Identify with Thoughts

Do you know the difference between a thought and thinking?

Imagine looking at clouds in the sky. Seeing them is like a thought. It just arises, drifts, and disappears. There is nothing you need to do.

But if you start asking questions, "Why is it cloudy? Why is it here again? Will it rain? Will it ruin my plans?" now you are thinking. You are engaging, analysing, judging, and predicting.

Your mind takes a simple observation and turns it into a chain of worries or mental loops. That's when a natural thought becomes a storm inside your head. Thinking becomes mental suffering when we identify with the thought.

Let's take another simple example. You are about to sleep, and a thought arises: "Did I lock the door?" That's just a thought. It came and could have passed.

But instead, the mind engages: "What if I didn't lock it? What if something happens? I should check again… just to be sure." Now the thought has grown into a loop, replaying itself in your mind.

Or imagine you see a friend driving a nice, expensive car. A thought arises: "Wow, that's a nice car." If you just notice it, it's neutral. It comes and goes.

But if you start engaging: "Why does he have this car and not me? What did he do differently? I'll never get that. Maybe I'm failing at life…" now a simple observation has turned into judgment, comparison, and self-criticism. The thought has grown into a story that can replay endlessly, stealing your energy and peace.

Most suffering doesn't come from the thoughts themselves, but from identifying with and engaging in them. A small worry arises, and before you know it, your mind declares, "I am anxious," "It's about me," or "I am failing." Instantly, that thought gains weight, authority, and control because a player called "me" or "I" has identified with it. What was once just a passing idea now feels like reality.

The root cause of the problem is not the thoughts, but the identity that you are the "thinker," and that the thoughts are yours. This is the trap. Not the thoughts, but you as the thinker.

This is identification. The act of taking a thought as you, as truth, as something that defines who you are or that it is about you. And it is one of the main engines of suffering. Identification fuels rumination, anxiety, OCD-like cycles, and even regret. The more we declare, "I am this thought," the more power we give it. Our own mind becomes a prison.

The thought gains power because we label it as "me" or "mine," as if it defines who we are. The mind starts weaving it into stories, loops, and compulsions. Anxiety, OCD, and rumination all thrive here.

The mind is trying to protect this sense of "me," this identity it has created. So every thought feels important, personal, and urgent. It reacts, analyses, and holds on, believing that something is at risk.

I used to believe every thought I had defined me. The thought became bigger than me. It controlled my mood, my energy, my day. My mind spiralled. I would replay every past mistake, imagine future disasters, and feel trapped in endless "what-ifs." Every attempt to fight it, control it, or analyse it made it stronger.

This is what makes obsessive thinking so cruel. It's not just the thought itself, it's the moment we claim it as us. The thought becomes the director of our mind, replaying the same story again and again.

I tried everything, fighting, reasoning, analysing, but the more I engaged, the stronger it became. I was exhausted, frustrated, and terrified of my own mind. This is the reality for anyone caught in obsessive, compulsive, or ruminative patterns. The suffering isn't in the thought itself; it's in claiming it as you.

We cannot stop our thoughts. They arise on their own. Even the Buddha did not teach that thoughts can be stopped completely. He pointed out that the mind is naturally restless and wandering. In the Dhammapada, it says: "*The mind is restless, difficult to guard and hard to control, wandering wherever it likes.*" (**Dhammapada 33**).

No one can fully control thoughts, not even the most awakened mind. What changes is not the disappearance of thoughts, but our relationship to them.

What we can control is whether we engage with those thoughts or whether we simply acknowledge them and allow them to subside.

I have learned this from observing my own patterns. When we don't identify with a thought, it arises, stays for a moment, and passes. Over time, if we do not engage with it or claim it as "me," it can even fade from memory. But when we claim ownership of a thought, the mind builds countless stories, mental loops, and endless searches for answers or verification. Those thoughts can replay for days, weeks, or even years.

What I have understood is this. The mind does not clearly know the difference between reality and illusion. Most of the thoughts we have are not real. They are mental formations, passing impressions.

But when we put effort into a simple thought, analysing it, judging it, or engaging with it, the mind begins to treat that illusion as reality.

And this is the root of much mental suffering.

What to Do When a Thought Arises

First, notice it. Simply become aware:

A thought has appeared.

Don't think, "I am having a thought." Instead, gently shift to:

A thought is arising.

Second, don't label it as good or bad. Don't say, "This is a bad thought," or "This means something about me." Just let it be.

Third, don't engage. Don't analyse it, don't judge it, don't fight it, and don't try to solve it. The more you engage, the more it grows. It's like fueling a fire while hoping it will stop.

Finally, let it pass. Just like clouds in the sky, thoughts come and go on their own if you don't hold on to them.

At first, this may feel difficult. The mind is used to reacting, controlling, and searching for answers. But with practice, something begins to change. You start to see thoughts for what they really are. Temporary, passing events, not truth, not identity, not you.

This is where freedom begins. Not by stopping thoughts, but by no longer being controlled by them.

A Simple Practice You Can Try

The next time a thought arises, pause for a moment.

Don't identify with it.

Don't label it as good or bad.

Don't try to fix it, fight it, or understand it.

Simply notice it.

Instead of thinking, "I am having a thought," gently shift to:

A thought is arising.

There is a thought… noticed.

Keep it simple. Keep it impersonal.

For a few seconds, maybe a minute, just stay with it. You don't have to do anything. You don't even need to understand it. Just observe. You may notice sensations in your body, or you may notice nothing at all. Both are okay.

Be aware that due to old patterns, habits, and cravings, the mind will try to trick you into engaging with the thought, often by creating a sense of fear, urgency, or danger. It may feel very real and convincing.

Don't react.

Allow the discomfort to be there. Feel it, and observe it as it is, without trying to escape or fix it.

And then something subtle but powerful begins to happen:

The mind starts to lose its urgency.

The need to fix, fight, or defend begins to fade.

The craving to engage weakens.

And without you forcing anything, the thought starts to dissolve on its own.

You didn't push it away.

You didn't solve it.

You simply didn't feed it.

The same applies not only to thoughts, but also to emotions.

The next time an emotion arises, whether it is worry, fear, or anger, pause for a moment.

Don't identify with it.

Don't label it as good or bad.

Don't try to fix it, fight it, or understand it.

Simply notice it.

Instead of saying, "I am angry," gently shift to:

Anger is arising.

There is anger… noticed.

Instead of "I am anxious," try:

Anxiety is present.

For a few seconds, maybe a minute, do nothing.

Don't react mentally.

Don't react physically.

Just observe.

You may feel sensations in your body, a tight chest, heat, restlessness, or tension. Stay with it. Don't run from it. Don't suppress it. Just watch.

And then something powerful begins to happen:

The emotion starts to lose its intensity.

The mind loses its urge to react, defend, or fix.

The wave begins to settle on its own.

You didn't suppress it.

You didn't express it.

You simply observed it.

And because you didn't feed it, it begins to fade.

This is the wisdom of the mind and body. Everything that

arises will pass if you don't hold on to it.

In that small pause, you are no longer controlled by the thought or emotion.

With every small moment of practice, something begins to change. The mind slowly learns a new way. The old habit of reacting, looping, and identifying starts to weaken. The more you observe without engaging, the less power thoughts and emotions have over you.

What once felt overwhelming begins to loosen its grip. What once controlled you begins to fade.

This is how the mind relearns. This is how it unwires itself, gently, naturally, through awareness.

Key Insight

The key is simple:
Thoughts and emotions are not the problem.
Identifying with them is.
When you stop claiming them as "me" or "mine,"
they lose their power.
And in that space...
peace was always there.

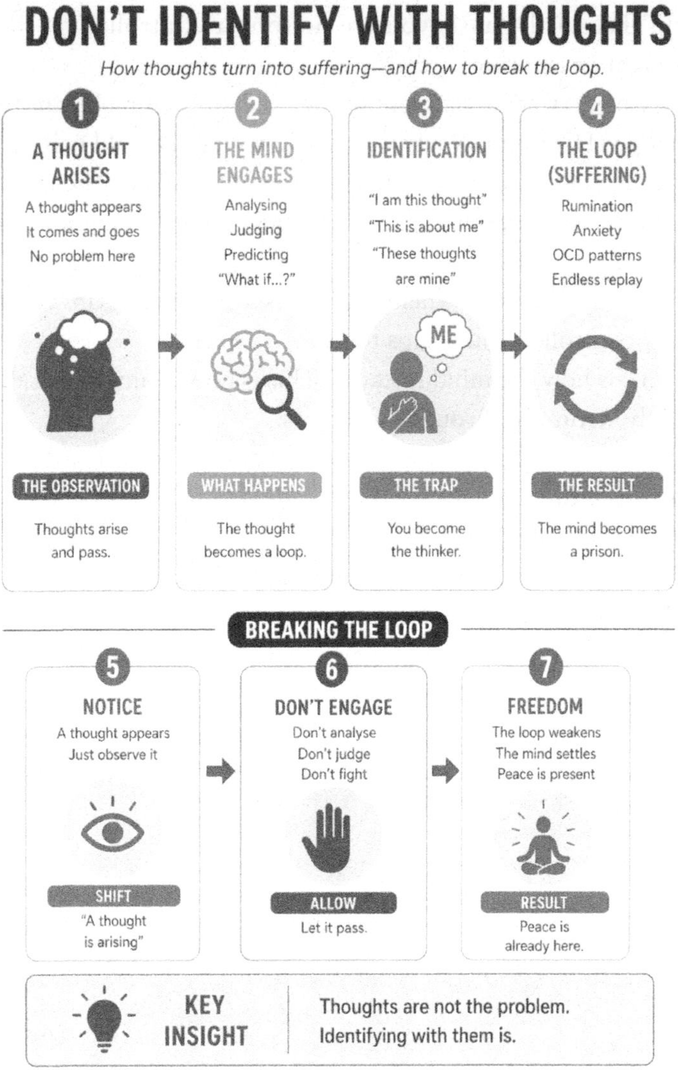
DON'T IDENTIFY WITH THOUGHTS
How thoughts turn into suffering—and how to break the loop.
1
A THOUGHT ARISES
A thought appears
It comes and goes
No problem here
THE OBSERVATION
Thoughts arise and pass.
2
THE MIND ENGAGES
Analysing
Judging
Predicting
"What if...?"
WHAT HAPPENS
The thought becomes a loop.
3
IDENTIFICATION
"I am this thought"
"This is about me"
"These thoughts are mine"
ME
THE TRAP
You become the thinker.
4
THE LOOP (SUFFERING)
Rumination
Anxiety
OCD patterns
Endless replay
THE RESULT
The mind becomes a prison.
BREAKING THE LOOP
5
NOTICE
A thought appears
Just observe it
SHIFT
"A thought is arising"
6
DON'T ENGAGE
Don't analyse
Don't judge
Don't fight
ALLOW
Let it pass.
7
FREEDOM
The loop weakens
The mind settles
Peace is present
RESULT
Peace is already here.
KEY INSIGHT
Thoughts are not the problem.
Identifying with them is.

18

Thoughts Have No Owner

If thoughts are not you, then whose are they?

When a thought arises, fear, doubt, anger, or desire, it feels personal. It feels like your thought. You say, "I am thinking this," or "This is happening to me."

But pause for a moment and look closely.

Did you choose this thought to appear?

Did you invite it?

Did you decide its content?

Can you control the thought?

Or did it simply arise on its own?

Thoughts come and go, just like sounds, sensations, or weather. You hear a sound, you don't say, "I created that sound." You feel the wind, you don't say, "This wind belongs to me."

As you look at the clouds, you don't know who owns them, where they came from, why they are here, or where they are going.

As you look at a river flowing, you don't ask, "Who owns this river?" It flows on its own, moving, changing, never staying the same. You don't control its direction or its speed. You simply observe it.

In the same way, thoughts arise in the mind. They are experienced, but not owned.

For example, you are sitting quietly, and suddenly a thought appears: "What if something goes wrong tomorrow?" You didn't plan it. You didn't choose it. It just appeared.

But the moment you say, "My worry… my fear…" you take ownership. And with that ownership comes anxiety, pressure, and the need to fix it.

Do Thoughts Really Belong to You?

The Buddha pointed to this through the understanding of non-self, that nothing that arises in the mind is truly "me" or "mine." Thoughts arise due to causes and conditions: past experiences, habits, memory, and the natural activity of the mind. They are events, not identity.

The Buddha explains that what arises and passes cannot be taken as "This is mine, this I am, this is my self." This insight applies not only to the body, but also to feelings, perceptions, and mental formations, including thoughts.

"Whatever is not yours, abandon it. When you have abandoned it, that will lead to your welfare and happiness. And what is not yours? Form is not yours... feeling is not yours... perception is not yours... mental formations are not yours... consciousness is not yours." (**Anattalakkhana Sutta (SN 22.59**)

Thoughts are part of these mental formations. They arise and pass. They are not "you," and they are not "yours."

So why does it feel like thoughts are ours?

Because the mind automatically labels them:

"My thought"

"My fear"

"My problem"

The moment this happens, the thought becomes personal. And once it becomes personal, the mind feels the need to protect it, solve it, fight it, or hold on to it.

This is how suffering begins.

Take a simple example. A thought arises: "I might fail."

If you take ownership:

"I might fail → I am not capable → I am a failure."

Now it becomes identity. Now it hurts.

But if you don't take ownership:

"A thought of failure is arising."

It stays as a thought. It doesn't become you. It passes.

The next time a thought arises, try this. Notice it: "A thought is arising." Don't say, "My thought." Don't say, "This is me." Just observe it as something appearing in the mind, like a sound, like a sensation, something experienced, not owned.

And notice what begins to change.

The pressure reduces.

The urgency fades.

The emotional charge weakens.

The mind no longer feels responsible to fix every thought. And slowly, thoughts begin to lose their grip.

Look closely again.

If you did not create the thought,

if you cannot stop it from arising,

and if it disappears on its own,

then how can it belong to you?

A thought appears.

It stays for a moment.

It passes.

Where is the owner in this process?

Look closely.

Where is the owner in all of this?

A thought appears.

It is noticed.

And then it passes.

Where, in this entire process, is the "owner"?

There is only the appearance of a thought,

and the awareness that notices it.

Nothing else.

Take a moment and observe this in your own experience.

A disturbing thought suddenly appears out of nowhere:

"What if I hurt someone?"

You didn't choose it.

You didn't want it.

It just appeared.

But instantly, the mind reacts:

"Why would I think this?"

"What does this say about me?"

"Am I a bad person?"

Now look closely.

The thought came first.

The fear came after.

The identity came after.

The mind created the owner.

Or you're going about your day, and suddenly a memory appears, something you said years ago.

Immediately, the mind says:

"That was so embarrassing."

"I shouldn't have done that."

"I am so stupid."

But pause.

Did you choose that memory to arise at that moment?

Or did it just appear?

The memory came first.

Then the "me" stepped in and turned it into identity.

The idea of "my thought" comes later. It is something the mind creates afterward. It labels, claims, and personalises.

But if you slow down and observe carefully, you will see the thought came first, and the label came later.

The ownership is added after the fact.

In that moment of direct observation, before the label, there is no "me" in the thought. There is only thinking happening. There is only a thought appearing in awareness.

But the mind quickly steps in and says:

"This is my thought."

"This is happening to me."

"This means something about me."

And the moment that happens, the illusion of an owner is created.

But in reality, there is no owner.

Thoughts arise due to conditions: memory, habit, experience, and the natural activity of the mind. Just like a sound arises when there is movement, or a wave forms when there is wind, thoughts arise when conditions are present.

They are happening, but not owned.

You don't create each thought.

You don't control when it appears.

You don't decide how long it stays.

It comes.

It is noticed.

It goes.

So if thoughts are not yours,

then who is aware of them?

Who is noticing them?

There is something here that sees the thought without being the thought, something that is aware, yet untouched.

That is what we will explore next.

Stay with that question.

Don't answer it yet. Just observe.

19

You Are the Witness

If thoughts are not yours, and thoughts have no owner, then who is aware of them?

Right now, as you read these words, thoughts may be arising. You may agree, disagree, question, or reflect. But pause for a moment and notice something subtle.

There is something in you that is aware of these thoughts and emotions.

Thoughts are changing. Emotions are also changing. They come and go. But this awareness remains.

Think about this.

A thought appears: "I am tired."

Then another: "I should do something."

Then another: "This is interesting."

Each thought is different. Each one comes and goes.

But something is constant. Something is noticing all of them.

That something is not a thought, because it is aware of thoughts.

That is you, the witness.

You are not the thought. You are not the owner of the

thought. You are the one who sees the thought.

Just like your eyes can see objects but are not the objects, in the same way, awareness can observe thoughts but is not the thoughts. And that awareness always remains within us, pure and clear, never defiled by past mistakes or future worries.

Just like the sky, awareness remains. What is changing and moving are the clouds, the weather, and everything within them.

Let's look at a simple example.

You are sitting quietly, and a thought arises: "I feel anxious."

If you identify with it, you say: "I am anxious."

But if you observe it, you notice: "There is anxiety being noticed."

Something is aware of the anxiety.

That awareness is calm. It is not anxious.

Another example.

You feel anger rising. Your body becomes tense. Your mind starts reacting. In that moment, it feels like: "I am angry."

But if you pause and observe, you may notice:

Anger is present.

It is being felt.

It is being observed.

And the moment you see it clearly, something shifts.

There is anger, and there is the awareness of anger.

They are not the same.

The Buddha pointed to this through direct observation, not by belief, but by experience.

Thoughts, emotions, and sensations arise and pass. But awareness, the knowing of them, remains steady. It does not come and go with every thought. It is already here.

"In the seen, there is only the seen; in the heard, there is only the

heard; in the sensed, there is only the sensed; in the cognized, there is only the cognized." **(Bahiya Sutta, Udana 1.10)**

There is no "me" inside it. There is no owner behind it.

It is just an experience happening.

So who are you?

Are you the thoughts that keep changing?

Or are you the one who notices them?

When you begin to rest as the witness, something powerful happens.

You no longer get pulled into every thought. You no longer react to every emotion.

There is space.

Thoughts still arise. Emotions still arise. But they don't control you in the same way, because you are no longer inside them. You are aware of them.

This does not mean thoughts disappear. It means your relationship with them changes.

You stop being the actor in every mental story and become the observer of the mind itself.

At first, this may feel unfamiliar. The mind is used to identifying, reacting, and controlling.

But with practice, the witness becomes clearer.

You begin to notice thoughts earlier. You begin to see emotions without being consumed by them. And slowly, a quiet sense of stability appears.

This awareness is not something you need to create.

It is already there. You are already aware, right now.

The only shift is recognising it.

The next time a thought arises, try this.

Instead of following it, pause.

Notice: "A thought is being seen."

Instead of saying, "I am anxious," try: "Anxiety is being observed."

And then stay there, just for a moment.

As the one who is aware.

You may notice something surprising.

The thought begins to lose its intensity.

The emotion begins to soften.

Not because you forced it, but because you are no longer entangled in it.

You are the witness.

The silent awareness behind every thought, every feeling, every experience.

Thoughts come and go.

Emotions rise and fall.

But the one who sees them remains.

And when you begin to live from that place, the mind no longer feels like a prison. It becomes something you can observe without being trapped inside it.

This is not the end of the journey.

It is the beginning of true clarity.

20

Observing Without Attachment

Now that you have seen that you are not your thoughts, and that you are the one who is aware of them, the next step is simple, but powerful.

Can you observe everything that arises without attaching to it?

Every day, thoughts and emotions continue to appear. A worry arises. A memory returns. An emotion builds. This will not stop. But what can change is how you relate to what appears.

Most of the time, the mind does one of two things: it holds on, or it pushes away. If something feels good, we want to keep it. If something feels uncomfortable, we want to get rid of it. This is attachment. And this is where suffering begins.

Imagine holding a handful of sand. If you hold it gently, it stays. If you grip it tightly, it slips through your fingers. The mind works the same way. The more you cling to thoughts and emotions, the more restless and unstable you feel.

Observing without attachment means something very simple: let things be.

When a thought arises, you don't chase it. When an emotion appears, you don't resist it. You just observe.

Thoughts are like clouds, and emotions are like the weather passing through the sky. They come and go on their own. You are like the sky, awareness that remains still and unchanged. You don't need to chase the clouds or push them away. Just watch them pass.

For example, a thought appears: "What if something goes wrong?" Instead of following it, you notice, "A thought is arising." And you let it pass.

An emotion may arise, such as anger, fear, or sadness. Instead of reacting, suppressing, or expressing it immediately, you pause. You feel it. You observe it without adding a story, without saying, "This shouldn't be here."

You receive a message that bothers you. A reaction rises instantly: anger, frustration, or hurt. The mind wants to react: reply immediately, defend yourself, replay the situation again and again. But now, try something different.

Pause.

Notice: "Anger is arising."

Feel it in your body, heat, tension, restlessness. Don't act. Don't suppress. Just observe.

Watch what happens.

The intensity begins to change. The urge to react weakens. And after some time, the emotion settles on its own.

At another moment, a strong urge appears: "I need to check my phone." "I need to know what's happening." "I can't sit still." It feels urgent. It feels like you must act.

But pause.

Did you choose that urge to appear? Or did it arise on its own?

Instead of acting, just observe: "An urge is present."

Feel it in the body, the pull, the restlessness, the discomfort. Stay with it. Watch carefully.

Without feeding it, the urge rises, peaks, and then fades.

You didn't satisfy it. You didn't fight it. You simply didn't attach to it.

At first, this may feel uncomfortable. The mind is used to reacting. It wants to fix, solve, escape, or control. But when you stay with the experience without attachment, something begins to change.

The thought fades. The emotion softens. Not because you forced it, but because you didn't hold onto it.

Everything that arises passes. This is the truth of impermanence.

A feeling comes. It stays for a moment. It goes.

A thought appears. It lingers. It disappears.

When you stop interfering, you begin to see this clearly.

This is observing without attachment.

You are not controlled by what arises.

This does not mean you become passive or inactive. It means you respond with clarity, not reaction. You act when needed, but not from impulse.

With practice, this becomes natural. You begin to create space between the thought and your response, the emotion and your action. And in that space, there is freedom.

The more you practice this, the more the mind learns. Old habits of reacting and clinging begin to weaken. You don't get pulled into every thought. You don't get consumed by every emotion.

Life continues. But your experience of it changes.

You begin to move through thoughts and emotions without

being trapped by them.

This is the beginning of a calm and steady mind.

Not because nothing arises, but because nothing is held onto.

And in that letting go, peace quietly reveals itself.

From Thought to Freedom

Over the last four chapters, we have explored a simple but powerful shift in understanding. We began by seeing that thoughts are not the problem, but identifying with them is. Then we looked deeper and saw that thoughts have no real owner. From there, we discovered that there is an awareness within us that notices thoughts and emotions without being affected by them.

And finally, we learned that by observing everything that arises without attachment, the mind begins to settle naturally. What once felt overwhelming starts to lose its grip. This is not about controlling the mind, but understanding it clearly. And in that understanding, a quiet sense of freedom begins to appear.

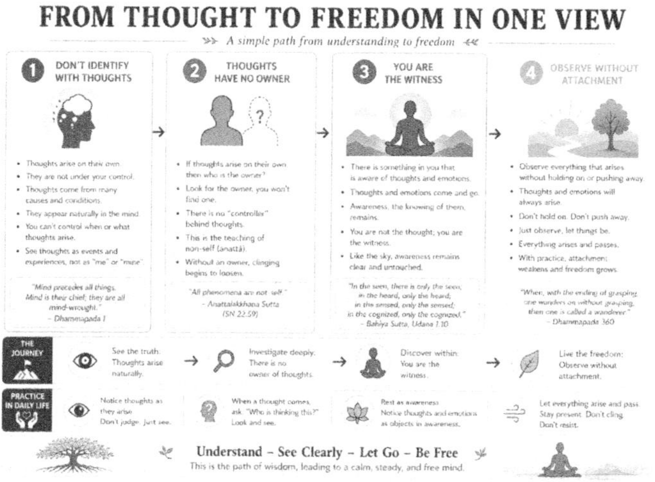
FROM THOUGHT TO FREEDOM IN ONE VIEW
A simple path from understanding to freedom
1 DON'T IDENTIFY WITH THOUGHTS
Thoughts arise on their own.
They are not under your control.
Thoughts come from many causes and conditions.
They appear naturally in the mind.
You can't control when or what thoughts arise.
See thoughts as events and experiences, not as "me" or "mine".
"Mind precedes all things. Mind is their chief; they are all mind-wrought." - Dhammapada 1
2 THOUGHTS HAVE NO OWNER
If thoughts arise on their own then who is the owner?
Look for the owner, you won't find one.
There is no "controller" behind thoughts.
This is the teaching of non-self (anattā).
Without an owner, clinging begins to loosen.
"All phenomena are not self." - Anattalakkhana Sutta (SN 22.59)
3 YOU ARE THE WITNESS
There is something in you that is aware of thoughts and emotions.
Thoughts and emotions come and go.
Awareness, the knowing of them, remains.
You are not the thought; you are the witness.
Like the sky, awareness remains clear and untouched.
"In the seen, there is only the seen; in the heard, only the heard; in the sensed, only the sensed; in the cognized, only the cognized." - Bahiya Sutta, Udana 1.10
4 OBSERVE WITHOUT ATTACHMENT
Observe everything that arises without holding on or pushing away.
Thoughts and emotions will always arise.
Don't hold on. Don't push away.
Just observe, let things be.
Everything arises and passes.
With practice, attachment weakens and freedom grows.
"When, with the ending of grasping one wanders on without grasping, then one is called a wanderer." - Dhammapada 360
THE JOURNEY
See the truth: Thoughts arise naturally.
Investigate deeply: There is no owner of thoughts.
Discover within: You are the witness.
Live the freedom: Observe without attachment.
PRACTICE IN DAILY LIFE
Notice thoughts as they arise. Don't judge. Just see.
When a thought comes, ask: "Who is thinking this?" Look and see.
Rest as awareness. Notice thoughts and emotions as objects in awareness.
Let everything arise and pass. Stay present. Don't cling. Don't resist.
Understand – See Clearly – Let Go – Be Free
This is the path of wisdom, leading to a calm, steady, and free mind.

21

Everything Changes (Anicca)

Now that you are beginning to observe thoughts and emotions without attachment, something deeper starts to become clear: everything changes.

At first, this may seem obvious. But when you truly look at your own experience, it becomes a powerful insight. A thought appears and then disappears. An emotion rises and then fades. A moment of joy comes and then passes. A difficult feeling arises, and eventually, it too changes. Nothing stays the same.

Look at your own day. You wake up with one mood, and it shifts. You feel stressed, then calm, then distracted, then focused. Even the strongest emotions do not remain forever.

Think about a moment when you felt anxious. At the time, it felt overwhelming, as if it would stay forever. But if you look back, that feeling changed. It did not stay the same. It rose, stayed for a while, and then faded.

Or think about a time when you were very happy. That moment also did not last forever. It came, it was felt, and then it passed.

Everything moves in this way.

And this is not limited to thoughts and emotions. If you look closely, everything in life is changing: situations, circumstances, and even people. Relationships evolve. People grow, drift apart, or move on. Even the way someone treats you can change over time. Nothing remains fixed.

Even your own life reflects this. Your job, your career, your priorities, they change. The person you were years ago is not the same person you are today. Even your body is changing moment by moment. Nothing you experience remains exactly as it is.

The problem is not that things change. The problem is that we expect them not to. We try to hold onto what feels good, and we try to push away what feels uncomfortable. But both are changing. And this is where suffering begins.

This is the nature of impermanence. Everything is changing, whether we want it to or not. And when we cling to what is impermanent, trying to hold it or push it away, we create suffering.

You may have noticed this in your own life. A strong thought can return again and again, but even that is not constant. It comes in waves. Sometimes it feels intense, and at other times it fades into the background. Even overthinking is not continuous. It rises, peaks, and then quiets down until it comes again.

Everything that arises passes.

In Buddhist wisdom, this is known as ***anicca***, the truth of impermanence, a cornerstone of the Buddha's teaching. It means that nothing in this world is permanent. Everything we see, everything we experience, thoughts, emotions, happiness, and suffering, is subject to change.

The Buddha pointed to this as a fundamental truth of life.

In the **Dhammapada 277**, it is said: *"All conditioned things are impermanent."*

This is not something to believe. It is something to see for yourself.

Everything that arises follows a natural process. It comes into being, remains for a time, changes, and eventually passes away. Nothing is exempt from this, not thoughts, not emotions, not relationships, not even our own bodies.

Anything that begins will also end. This is the nature of all experience.

In my own journey, understanding this changed something deeply. I used to believe that my thoughts, my feelings, and even my struggles were permanent. When anxiety came, it felt like it would never leave. When overthinking started, it felt endless. With OCD, it felt the same, it felt like it would never end, like it would keep going on and on, almost as if it would take over everything.

But as I began to observe more closely the nature of impermanence, I saw something different. Even the strongest thoughts would shift. Even the most intense emotions would fade. What felt permanent was not.

That realisation did not come from belief. It came from seeing it again and again. And slowly, something began to loosen. I stopped holding on so tightly. I stopped fearing every thought and every feeling, because I could see they were not staying.

Right now, notice what is happening. A thought may be present, a sensation in the body, or a feeling in the mind. Stay with it for a moment and watch carefully. It is already changing. Even if it feels strong, it is not fixed.

This is where freedom begins. When you see clearly that everything changes, you stop trying to control every experience. You do not need to hold onto thoughts, and you do not need to fight emotions, because you know they will pass.

This does not make you passive. It makes you clear. You still act and respond, but you are no longer driven by fear of losing or the need to control. You begin to trust the natural movement of experience.

Just like waves rise and fall in the ocean, and clouds move across the sky, everything comes and goes. Thoughts change. Emotions change. Situations change. But the one who notices them remains, that is, awareness.

The more you begin to see this, the lighter the mind becomes. You do not cling as tightly, and you do not resist as strongly. There is more space, and in that space, there is peace.

Not because life has stopped changing, but because you are no longer fighting that change.

This is the truth of impermanence: everything changes.

And when this is deeply understood, something softens within you. You stop holding on so tightly. You begin to let life move as it is.

And in that letting go, a quiet freedom begins to appear.

Understanding the Nature of Impermanence

It is important to understand the nature of impermanence. When this is seen clearly, it helps us make sense of life and embrace both its challenges and its moments of ease.

Much of our suffering comes from holding onto the illusion that things are permanent, that people, material possessions, achievements, happiness, and even sorrow will remain the same. But in reality, everything changes. And when we expect it not to, we create inner conflict.

We struggle because we are fighting the natural flow of life. We try to hold on to what cannot stay, and we resist what we cannot avoid. This constant tension between what is and what we want it to be is what creates suffering.

When you begin to accept the nature of impermanence, something shifts. There is less to fight, less to resist. The mind becomes lighter because it is no longer in conflict with reality.

You begin to let go of unrealistic expectations. You stop expecting life, people, or even yourself to remain fixed.

And with that, something beautiful happens.

You start to appreciate what is here, while it is here.

Moments of happiness are valued more deeply. Times of sorrow are understood rather than resisted. The people around you are seen with more presence and care because you know they, too, are changing, and that, like all things, they will not be here forever.

You may also notice something else. Understanding impermanence can soften the way you hold onto the past.

There may be people who hurt you years ago. The mind keeps replaying what happened, as if it is still present. But if you look closely, that moment has already passed. The person has changed. You have changed. The situation is no longer the same.

Holding onto that pain is like holding onto something that no longer exists in the same way.

In my own experience, this understanding helped me deeply. Much of my OCD, rumination, and overthinking was tied to the past, especially to people who had hurt me. The mind would replay those moments again and again, as if they were still happening.

But when I began to see the nature of impermanence, something shifted. Those moments were no longer here. The people had changed. I had changed. What I was holding onto was no longer the same reality.

Seeing this did not erase the past, but it loosened its grip. The thoughts came less often, and when they did, they did not carry the same weight. I did not feel the need to fight them or solve them anymore.

As this becomes clear, forgiveness begins to feel more natural, not forced or artificial. Not because what happened was right, but because you see that everything involved has already changed and is not permanent.

You begin to live more fully in the present moment, not because everything is perfect, but because you understand that nothing stays.

And in that understanding, there is peace.

A Simple Practice You Can Try

The next time a thought or emotion arises, pause for a moment.

Notice it clearly:

A thought is present.

A feeling is here.

Instead of reacting, just observe.

Watch what happens.

Does it stay the same, or does it begin to change?

Stay with it for a few seconds, or a minute if you can. You don't need to do anything. Just notice how it shifts, moves, and eventually fades.

You may feel an urge to hold on or push it away. Notice that too.

See how even that urge changes.

Keep it simple.

You are not trying to control the experience. You are simply watching the natural process of change.

And as you continue to observe, you may begin to see this clearly:

Nothing stays.

Everything is moving, changing, and passing.

22

There Is No Fixed Self (Anatta)

If everything is changing or impermanent, then what exactly is "me"?

We often feel that there is a solid, fixed self behind our thoughts and experiences. We say, "This is me," "This is my thought," "This is my feeling." It feels personal, real, and constant. But if you look closely, is it really so?

The idea of a fixed "me" or "I" is often a mental construct, a story we tell ourselves. The belief that there is a solid, unchanging self is a misunderstanding and one of the root causes of suffering. Accepting that there is no solid or permanent self is a path to liberation and peace.

As the Buddha taught in the **Dhammapada**: *"All phenomena are not-self. When one sees this with wisdom, one turns away from suffering. This is the path to purification."* (**Dhammapada 279**)

A thought appears, and then it disappears. An emotion arises, and then it fades. A belief you once held strongly may change over time. Even your personality shifts depending on situations, people, and stages of life. So what exactly remains the same?

In Buddhist wisdom, this is explored through the understanding of ***anatta***, often translated as "no self." It does not mean that you do not exist. It means that there is no fixed, permanent, unchanging identity behind your experiences.

The Buddha pointed to this clearly in the **Anattalakkhana Sutta (SN 22.59)**. He taught that what we call "self" is made up of changing processes: body, feelings, perceptions, mental formations, and consciousness. And of these, he said: *"This is not mine, this I am not, this is not my self."* (**Anattalakkhana Sutta, SN 22.59**)

Each of these elements arises, changes, and passes away. None of them remains fixed. And if they are changing, they cannot be who you truly are.

Look at your own experience. Are you the same person you were ten years ago? Even five years ago? Your thoughts have changed. Your preferences have changed. Your reactions have changed.

Even within a single day, you are not the same. In one moment you feel calm, in another restless, in another joyful, in another irritated. If the "self" keeps changing, can it really be a fixed identity?

What we call "self" is often just a collection of thoughts, memories, and patterns held together by the mind. It creates a story: "This is who I am." But that story is constantly being updated, revised, and reshaped. And yet, we hold onto it as if it is solid.

This is where suffering deepens.

When we believe in a fixed self, every thought becomes personal. Every emotion feels like "me." Every criticism feels like an attack on who we are. Every fear becomes something we must protect against.

But if there is no fixed self, then what is there to defend?

A thought arises, it is not you. An emotion appears; it is not you. A memory surfaces, it is not you. They are experiences, not identity.

Understanding this does not remove life; it brings freedom into it.

When there is less attachment to a fixed "me," there is less fear, less defensiveness, and less pressure to control everything. You no longer feel the need to protect an image of yourself. You begin to respond more naturally, more openly.

Even difficult thoughts lose some of their power, because they are no longer seen as "who you are," but simply as something passing through the mind.

In my own experience, this understanding changed the way I related to my thoughts. Many of my struggles came from taking thoughts personally, believing they said something about me. But when I began to see that thoughts arise on their own and are not a fixed self, something shifted.

There was less need to fight them, less need to prove or defend anything, and less fear of what a thought might mean. The mind became quieter, not because thoughts stopped, but because they were no longer taken as "me."

This does not mean you become empty or disconnected. It means you become free.

Free from the constant pressure of maintaining an identity. Free from being pulled into every thought and emotion. Free to experience life without turning everything into "me" and "mine."

So the next time a thought arises, pause for a moment.

Instead of saying, "This is me," notice: "This is a thought."

Instead of saying, "I am this," notice: "This is being experienced."

And stay with that.

Because when the idea of a fixed self begins to loosen, something else becomes clear. There is experience, but no solid owner behind it.

And in that space, there is a different kind of freedom.

Why Understanding Anatta (No Fixed Self) Matters

Understanding *anatta,* that there is no fixed, solid self, is deeply important. It helps you see that what you call "I" is not a permanent identity, but a flow of changing experiences.

This understanding loosens attachment to identity and ego. You no longer feel the same need to define, protect, or defend yourself. It reduces clinging and aversion. You are less attached to what you like and less resistant to what you dislike. And because of this, it brings a deep sense of peace and freedom.

This is especially powerful for those who struggle with mental patterns such as OCD, overthinking, anxiety, or rumination. When there is a strong sense of "me," every thought feels personal. The mind keeps asking, "Why did I think this? What does this say about me? What if this thought is true?" But when you begin to see that thoughts are not a fixed self, something shifts. The thought is no longer "me." It is just a thought. And because of this, the intensity begins to reduce. The need to analyse, fix, or fight every thought weakens. There is space.

This understanding also helps in how you relate to the past. There may be people who mistreated you or hurt you deeply. The pain often continues because the mind holds onto a fixed identity: "This happened to me," "I was treated this way," "This defines me." But when you see that both you and the other person are changing, something softens. The past is no longer the same reality. What you are holding onto is not fixed; it has already changed. This does not justify what happened, but it loosens its grip.

The same is true in relationships. Sometimes people do not love you the same way they once did. They may not show the same care, attention, or appreciation. This creates pain because we expect things to remain as they were. But when you understand impermanence and no fixed self, you begin to see that people change, feelings change, and relationships change. The version of the person you once knew is not exactly the same now.

When you stop expecting people to remain the same, there is less hurt, less resistance, and more acceptance. You begin to relate to people as they are now, not as they were. From this, a different kind of love begins to emerge, one that is more natural, more kind, and less conditional. You are no longer loving people based on who they used to be or who you expect them to be, but for who they are in this moment.

This understanding removes the need to control or hold onto others. It softens expectations and reduces the pressure we place on people to behave in certain ways or remain the same. In that space, love becomes lighter, more open, and free from control.

Many people are consumed by the need to define themselves. They attach their identity to their profession, possessions, relationships, or social status. When something affects these, they feel lost, disappointed, or even broken. But when you understand *anatta,* you begin to see that there is no fixed "me" to protect or defend. There is only a continuous flow of experiences.

And in seeing this clearly, something releases.

You no longer carry the same burden of identity.

And in that release, there is freedom.

A Simple Practice You Can Try

The next time a thought arises, pause for a moment.

Notice it clearly:

A thought is present.

Instead of saying, "This is me," gently shift to:

"This is a thought."

Stay with it.

Watch what happens.

Does the thought stay the same, or does it begin to change?

Now look a little deeper.

Where is the "me" in this thought?

Is it in the words?

Is it in the feeling?

Or is it something the mind adds afterwards?

Stay with that question for a few moments, without trying to answer it.

Just observe.

You may begin to notice that the thought is simply appearing, being noticed, and then passing.

There is experience… but no solid owner behind it.

Keep it simple.

You are not trying to remove the thought. You are not trying to find an answer.

You are simply seeing clearly what is already happening.

And as you continue to observe in this way, something begins to loosen.

The sense of "me" around the thought becomes lighter.

The need to defend, analyse, or control begins to fade.

And in that space, there is a quiet sense of freedom.

23

The Two Arrows: Why We Suffer Twice

Now that you have begun to see that thoughts are not "you," that they are not permanent, and that there is no fixed self behind them, something important becomes easier to understand: not all suffering is the same.

Some pain is natural, but much of our suffering is created by the mind.

The Buddha explained this through an analogy found in the **Sallatha Sutta (SN 36.6)**. He described how an ordinary person, when experiencing pain, is like someone struck by an arrow. This represents the first kind of pain, the natural pain of life, such as physical discomfort, loss, or emotional hurt.

He then explained that the person reacts with sorrow, distress, and mental struggle, creating a second layer of suffering. As the teacher says: "*When touched by a painful feeling, the uninstructed person sorrows, grieves, and laments... he feels two pains, physical and mental.*" **(SN 36.6)**

This is often described as being struck by two arrows.

The first arrow is unavoidable. It is part of being human.

Pain and discomfort are universal.

But the second arrow is created by the mind.

When something painful happens, the mind begins to react. It asks, "Why did this happen to me? This shouldn't be happening. What does this mean about me? How do I fix this? This will never go away."

This is the second arrow.

It is not the original pain, it is the mental reaction to it.

And often, this second arrow causes more suffering than the first.

The first arrow may be a moment of pain, but the second arrow turns it into ongoing suffering.

For example, a difficult thought arises. That is the first arrow. But then the mind reacts: "Why am I thinking this? What does this say about me? I need to get rid of this." Now the suffering increases.

Or someone says something hurtful. That is the first arrow. But then the mind keeps replaying it: "They shouldn't have said that. I can't believe this happened. This always happens to me." Now the pain continues long after the moment has passed.

This becomes even clearer in deeper life situations, moments that affect people emotionally.

A relationship ends, or someone breaks your trust. That is the first arrow. But then the mind keeps going: "Why did this happen to me? What did I do wrong? I'll never find someone again. My life is ruined." Now the pain turns into ongoing suffering.

Someone you care about pulls away or becomes distant. That is the first arrow. But then the mind says, "They don't value me. I'm not important. I must have done something wrong."

Now the mind creates a story that deepens the hurt.

You are rejected by a person, a job, or an opportunity. That is the first arrow. But then the mind adds, "I'm not good enough. I'll never succeed. This always happens to me." Now the moment begins to define you.

You feel like you failed at something important in life. That is the first arrow. But then the mind keeps repeating it: "I've wasted my time. I've ruined everything. It's too late for me." Now the suffering becomes heavy and long-lasting.

You experience loss of a person, a relationship, or something meaningful. That is the first arrow. But then the mind resists it: "This shouldn't have happened. I can't accept this. I won't be okay without this." Now the pain becomes harder to carry.

In all these situations, the first arrow is real. The pain is real.

But the second arrow, the mental story, the repetition, the resistance, is what turns pain into prolonged suffering.

You do not have to keep shooting yourself with the second arrow.

You do not have to torture yourself or let one moment define your life.

Daily examples make this even clearer.

You make a small mistake at work. That is the first arrow. But then the mind adds, "I'm not good enough. What will others think? I always mess things up. Am I in trouble? Will I lose my job?" Now the suffering grows.

A painful memory from the past comes up. That is the first arrow. But then the mind starts replaying it, analysing it, judging it, and trying to fix it. Now the past becomes present suffering.

Someone does not reply to your message. That is the first arrow. But then the mind says, "Did I say something wrong?

Are they ignoring me? Maybe they don't like me anymore." Now the mind creates a story, and the suffering begins.

Someone criticises you or speaks harshly. That is the first arrow. But then the mind keeps replaying it: "How dare they say that? I should have responded differently. I can't let this go." Now the moment lives on inside you.

The moment continues long after it has passed, robbing you of present peace and clarity.

The same happens with anxiety, regret, and overthinking. A feeling arises, that is natural. But then the mind resists it, fears it, or tries to control it. This creates the second arrow.

This is where most suffering comes from, not from what happens, but from how the mind reacts to what happens.

Understanding this changes everything.

You may not always be able to avoid the first arrow. Life will still bring challenges, loss, discomfort, and uncertainty.

But the second arrow is something you can begin to see.

And when you see it clearly, something shifts. You begin to notice the moment the mind reacts. You begin to see how thoughts build on top of each other. You begin to recognise that the suffering is being created in real time.

And in that moment of awareness, there is a choice.

You do not have to add the second arrow.

You do not have to create more suffering.

Instead of reacting, you can pause. Instead of resisting, you can observe. Instead of asking, "Why is this happening to me?" you can notice, "This is what is here right now."

This connects directly with what you have already seen. A thought is not you. There is no fixed self behind it. So there is nothing that needs to be defended.

This does not remove the first arrow, but it prevents the

suffering from multiplying.

In my own experience, this understanding was very important. Much of my struggle with overthinking, OCD, and mental loops came from the second arrow. The original thought or feeling was not the problem, it was the reaction to it.

But when I began to see this clearly, the cycle started to weaken. The thought would arise, but I did not immediately react. The feeling would come, but I did not add more fear or resistance.

And because of this, the intensity began to reduce. The mind became quieter, not because life became perfect, but because I stopped adding unnecessary suffering to what was already there.

This is the freedom in understanding the two arrows.

Pain may still arise, but suffering does not have to continue. Pain is part of life, but the suffering created by the mind is optional.

A Simple Practice: Seeing the Two Arrows

When you are struck by the first arrow, pain, discomfort, loss, or emotional hurt, just notice it.

Acknowledge it.

Accept it.

Do not resist it.

Observe it as it is.

Then watch carefully.

When you feel yourself being struck by the second arrow, the mental reaction, the overthinking, the fear, bring awareness to it.

Pause and gently ask, “Do I really need to be hit by the second arrow?"

You do not need to fight the thought.

You do not need to get rid of it.

Just see it for what it is, a reaction.

The moment you see it clearly, something loosens.

With practice, this becomes easier. Each time you notice the second arrow and do not follow it, the mind begins to lose its habit of creating extra suffering.

Over time, the first arrow may still come, but the second arrow begins to fade.

Life shoots the first arrow. The mind shoots the second.

24

Why It Still Feels Like There Is a "Me"

Now that you have seen how suffering is created through the second arrow, something deeper begins to reveal itself.

Why does the mind react in the first place?

Why does a simple thought or feeling turn into something personal?

The answer lies in something we rarely question: the sense of "me."

The mind is constantly creating a story about who you are, what has happened to you, and what it all means. This story is built from memories, experiences, beliefs, and roles you have taken on over time.

"I am this kind of person."

"This is what happened to me."

"This is who I should be."

These are not fixed truths, they are interpretations. But over time, they begin to feel real.

You begin to live through this story.

And once this sense of "me" is formed, everything becomes personal. A thought is no longer just a thought, it becomes my thought. An emotion is no longer just a feeling, it becomes my pain. A situation is no longer just an event, it becomes something happening to me.

This is how the sense of "me" is created and strengthened.

You are not just experiencing life, you are interpreting it through a story. And then you begin to defend that story.

If someone says something that does not match your identity, you feel hurt. If something challenges your beliefs, you feel uncomfortable. If life does not go the way your story expects, you feel frustrated.

Not because of what happened, but because it conflicts with the idea of "me."

This is where attachment begins.

You become attached to roles such as "I am successful," "I am not good enough," or "I am the one who was hurt." You become attached to past experiences, "This happened to me, so this is who I am." You become attached to future expectations, "This is how my life should be."

And the more you hold onto these, the more suffering is created.

Because life does not stay fixed.

People change. Situations change. You change.

But the mind tries to keep the story the same.

This creates tension, conflict, and suffering.

In reality, what you call "me" is not a fixed identity. It is a collection of changing thoughts, memories, and roles. It is something the mind creates and continues to update.

And yet, it feels solid.

This is the illusion.

In my own experience, I could see how much of my overthinking and emotional struggle came from this. It was not just the thoughts themselves, but the meaning I gave them about "me."

A thought would arise, and instantly it would connect to identity: "What does this say about me? Why am I like this? This is who I am." And that is where the suffering deepened.

But when I began to see that this "me" is a story, not something fixed, something began to loosen.

The thought was just a thought.

The feeling was just a feeling.

It did not have to define me.

And because of that, there was less to defend, less to hold onto, and less to protect.

This does not mean you stop functioning in the world.

You still have roles.

You still have responsibilities.

You still live your life.

But you no longer become trapped in the story.

You begin to see the difference between what is happening and the story about what is happening.

Try to notice this directly.

Right now, a thought may appear about "me."

Pause and look closely.

Is it something solid, or just a thought being noticed?

And in that space, something opens.

You can respond without being controlled by identity. You can experience life without constantly turning everything into "me" and "mine."

This is where a deeper freedom begins.

25

The Space Between Thought and Reaction

After seeing how thoughts are not you, how everything changes, how there is no fixed self, and how suffering is created through the second arrow, something important begins to become visible.

There is a space, a very small space. It exists between a thought arising and your reaction to it.

At first, it is almost impossible to notice. The mind moves so quickly that everything feels immediate. A thought appears, and the reaction follows instantly. It feels automatic, as if there is no gap at all.

But when you begin to observe more carefully, something changes. You start to notice that a thought appears, and before you react, there is a moment of awareness. It may be very brief. It may feel subtle. But it is there.

And in that moment, something important becomes possible.

You are no longer completely controlled by the thought. You begin to see it. Instead of being pulled into it immediately, you are aware of it. And in that awareness, there is a choice.

You do not have to follow the thought. You do not have to react in the same way. You do not have to create the second arrow.

This is where everything you have learned begins to come together. A thought arises, that is natural. A feeling appears, that is part of life. But what happens next is not fixed.

For example, a thought appears: "Something is wrong." Before, the mind would react instantly. It would analyse, worry, and try to fix the problem. One thought would lead to another, and the cycle would continue.

But now, something different can happen.

The thought appears, and you notice it. Instead of reacting, you pause. You see it as a thought, not as a fact, not as "you." And in that moment, the cycle weakens.

The same is true with emotions. A feeling of anxiety arises. Before, it would lead to resistance, fear, and overthinking. But now, you notice it. You feel it without immediately reacting to it. And in that space, the intensity begins to change.

This space is very powerful. It is not something you create, it is something you begin to notice. It has always been there, but the mind was moving too fast to see it. This is also where peace exists, not in controlling thoughts, but in the space before reacting to them.

With practice, this space becomes clearer. You begin to notice thoughts earlier. You begin to recognise reactions before they fully take over. You begin to feel emotions without being consumed by them.

And slowly, something shifts.

You are no longer living on automatic. You are no longer reacting to every thought and feeling. There is space, and in that space, there is freedom.

This does not mean you stop acting or responding. It means your actions come from clarity, not reaction. You still respond to life, but not from fear, not from habit, and not from the need to protect a fixed "me."

In my own experience, this was a turning point. Before, everything felt immediate. A thought would arise, and I was already inside it. A feeling would come, and I was already reacting.

But when I began to notice this space, even for a moment, something changed. I did not have to follow every thought. I did not have to react to every feeling. And that small shift made a big difference.

The mind became quieter, not because thoughts disappeared, but because I was no longer caught in every reaction.

This is where real change begins. Not by controlling thoughts. Not by forcing the mind to be silent. But by seeing clearly and allowing space.

The next time a thought arises, try this. Pause. Notice the moment before you react. Stay there, even if only for a second, and see what happens.

Because in that small space, there is more freedom and peace than you might expect.

26

Breaking the Cycle of Overthinking and OCD

Overthinking and OCD can feel overwhelming. Over time, they can begin to consume your life. Thoughts repeat, questions do not stop, and the mind keeps searching for answers, certainty, or relief. At times, it can feel like something is wrong with you.

But when you look more closely, something important becomes clear. The problem is not the thought. The problem is your relationship with the thought.

A thought appears, that is natural. Every mind produces thoughts. Some are random, some are uncomfortable, and some do not make sense. But what turns a simple thought into overthinking or OCD is what happens next. The mind reacts. It tries to understand the thought, solve it, or get rid of it. And in doing so, it gives the thought importance. The thought becomes something to fix.

This is where the cycle begins. A thought appears, the mind reacts, more thoughts follow, and more analysis begins. The loop continues. This is not because the thought is powerful, but because attention and belief are being added to it.

Another layer to this is the need for certainty. The mind wants to feel safe and have clear answers. It asks, "Is this true?" "What if this happens?" "What if I am wrong?" "Did I check the stove?" "Did I lock the door?" It keeps searching and checking.

For many people, this does not stop at thinking, it turns into action. You may check the door once, then again, and again. You may check the stove even when you know you already checked it. You may clean something repeatedly, even when it is already clean. You may replay conversations in your mind, trying to make sure everything was said correctly. In that moment, it feels necessary, as if you must do it to feel okay.

But what is really happening is this. A thought appears, anxiety rises, and you act to reduce that anxiety. For a moment, there is relief. But that relief is temporary. The mind quickly learns, "This action helped. Do it again." And so the cycle repeats. The thought returns, the anxiety rises again, and the urge to act becomes stronger. Over time, this pattern becomes automatic, not because you are weak, but because the mind is trying to protect you in the only way it knows.

But the more it searches, the more the doubt grows. Thoughts do not provide certainty. They only create more thinking.

This is where control comes in. The mind believes, "If I can just control this thought, I will feel better." So it tries to suppress the thought, replace it, analyse it, or avoid triggers. But this strengthens the cycle. Every attempt to control the thought sends a message: "This thought is important." And the mind holds onto it even more.

This is the root. Not the thought itself, but identification, fear, and the need to control. And as long as this pattern continues, the mind keeps repeating it again and again.

You have already seen this in earlier chapters. A thought is not you. There is no fixed self behind it. Not every thought needs a reaction. But when a thought is taken personally, "This is my thought, this says something about me," it becomes heavier. When fear is added, it becomes urgent. When control is added, it becomes persistent. And that is how overthinking and OCD patterns are formed.

In my own experience, this was a major shift. I used to believe that I needed to solve every thought, that if a thought appeared it meant something important, and that I had to understand it or fix it. But that only kept the cycle going. The more I engaged, the stronger it became.

What was even more painful was this. For years, I lived with OCD and overthinking. Every time a thought appeared, I would tell myself, "This is the last thought. This is the last ritual I'm doing." But sadly, years passed by. The most important part of life kept passing. And there was never a final thought to attend to.

When I began to step back, something changed. The thought would still appear, but I did not immediately react. I did not try to solve it or control it. Slowly, the intensity reduced, not because the thought disappeared, but because I stopped feeding it.

This is the key. Thoughts do not need to be controlled. They need to be seen.

When a thought arises, instead of reacting, simply notice it: "This is a thought." Nothing more. You do not need to answer it, fight it, or get rid of it. Let it be there.

At first, this may feel uncomfortable. The mind will still try to pull you in. It will say, "Just think about this one more time,"

"Just make sure," or "Just figure it out." But if you stay with awareness without reacting, something begins to shift.

The thought loses its grip. The loop weakens. Over time, the mind becomes quieter, not because thoughts stop, but because you are no longer caught in them.

This is not about forcing the mind to change. It is about understanding how the cycle works and no longer feeding it.

And when that happens, something important becomes possible.

Freedom from the loop.

When the Mind Stops Stirring

A simple way to understand overthinking and OCD is to imagine a glass of water with mud in it. If you keep stirring it, the water stays cloudy. You cannot see clearly.

This is what happens when you keep engaging with every thought, analysing, questioning, reacting. The more you try to figure it out, the more confused and overwhelmed you feel.

In OCD, this "stirring" often shows up as repeated checking, reassurance, or mental reviewing. In overthinking, it shows up as constant analysing and replaying. Different forms, but the same movement, continuous disturbance.

But if you put the glass down and leave it alone, something natural happens. The mud begins to settle. The water becomes clear on its own.

You did not force the clarity. You simply stopped disturbing it.

The mind works in the same way. When you stop interfering with every thought, when you stop trying to control, solve, or fix everything, the mental noise begins to settle.

At first, this feels uncomfortable. The urge to keep stirring is strong. But if you stay with awareness and do not react, the system begins to calm down on its own.

Clarity is not something you create. It is something that appears when the disturbance ends.

The Endless Search for Certainty

For OCD, it can be understood in another way. Imagine using a search engine to find certainty.

You type in a question, and it gives you answers. But along with those answers come more links, more possibilities, and more questions. You click one, then another, then another.

Instead of clarity, you begin to feel more unsure. So you search again, hoping this time you will find the final answer that settles everything.

But it never fully settles. Each answer creates more doubt. Because the mind is not designed to give certainty, it is designed to keep searching.

This is exactly how OCD operates. The mind asks, "Are you sure?" and you try to answer it. You check, you think, you analyse, or you seek reassurance. For a moment, there is relief.

But the relief does not last.

The question returns, often stronger than before.

Why? Because each time you search for certainty, you train the mind to keep asking. The cycle is strengthened, not resolved.

The way out is not to find the perfect answer.

It is to stop searching.

When the question arises, you allow it to be there without trying to solve it. No checking, no analysing, no reassurance.

At first, anxiety may rise. The mind will push harder.

But without your engagement, the cycle weakens.

Over time, the need for certainty begins to lose its grip.

The Tug of War

For overthinking, imagine you are in a tug of war, pulling hard on a rope. It feels intense, exhausting, and important, like you must win.

This is what happens when you try to fight your thoughts, control them, or figure everything out. You keep pulling, thinking more, analysing more, trying harder.

But then you realise something surprising. There is no one on the other end of the rope.

The struggle exists because you keep pulling.

The moment you let go, the tension disappears.

Overthinking works the same way. The effort to solve every thought, to reach a perfect answer, to mentally control every situation, that is what keeps the struggle alive.

Letting go does not mean giving up on life. It means dropping the unnecessary mental struggle.

You allow thoughts to come and go without getting involved in every one of them.

And when you stop pulling, the mind begins to settle.

Stepping Out of the Loop

The root of overthinking and OCD is not the thought. It is the reaction, the fear, and the need to control.

The way out is not to win the battle in the mind, but to step out of it. Because the moment you stop feeding the cycle, the mind loses its power to hold you.

In my own life, overthinking and OCD felt like a monster in my head. It took over my attention, my peace, and the quality of my life. The hardest part was this. People around me could see what I was doing, but I couldn't stop. The more I tried to fight it, the stronger it became. The more I tried to suppress it, the more intense it returned. The more I tried to escape it, the more it followed me. It felt powerful, almost impossible to overcome.

But over time, something became clear. This "monster" was not being fed by the thoughts themselves. It was being fed by my reaction to them. Every time I fought, analysed, checked, or tried to control, I was feeding the cycle. And that is why it kept growing.

This is why the usual approach does not work. Trying to stop OCD and overthinking by force keeps the mind in survival mode. The mind believes something is wrong, something must be fixed, something must be controlled. And the more you fight, the more you stay trapped in that state.

The shift begins when you move out of survival mode and into a state of safety. This does not happen by solving every thought or finding certainty. It happens when you allow thoughts to be there without reacting to them. When you stop treating every thought as a problem, the cycle begins to weaken.

This is what it means to starve the pattern. Not fighting it, not suppressing it, but no longer feeding it with fear, reaction, and control. And when you stop feeding it, something begins to change. What once felt like a powerful monster starts to lose its strength, not because you defeated it, but because you stopped giving it energy.

In many ways, this cycle works like an addiction.

A thought appears, anxiety rises, and the mind looks for relief. You check, analyse, or perform a ritual, and for a moment, the anxiety reduces. That relief feels real. It feels like something worked.

But that relief comes at a cost.

The mind learns from it. The mind is conditioned like that. It learns that the only way to feel safe is to react, to check, to think more. And so the next time a thought appears, the urge is stronger. The cycle repeats, not because the thought is stronger, but because the habit has been reinforced.

Just like any addiction, it is not the substance or the thought that keeps the cycle alive. It is the temporary relief that follows the action. That relief becomes the hook.

And the more you feed it, the more the mind depends on it.

At first, it feels like you are doing something to reduce anxiety. But over time, it becomes something you cannot stop. The mind keeps asking for more, more checking, more thinking, more certainty.

This is why the cycle feels so powerful.

But the way out is the same.

Not by forcing it to stop, but by no longer feeding it.

When the thought appears and you do not react, when the anxiety rises and you do not escape it, the pattern begins to weaken. The mind does not get the relief it is expecting, and slowly, it starts to unlearn the habit.

At first, this can feel uncomfortable. The urge is strong. The anxiety may rise even more. But if you stay with it, without feeding the cycle, something begins to change.

The pull becomes weaker. The urgency begins to fade. The mind starts to settle on its own.

And over time, what once felt like an addiction begins to lose its grip.

What once felt like a prison was only a loop you kept returning to. And when you begin to see it clearly, something shifts. You realise that the door was never locked, and you can walk out.

27

Letting Go Without Letting Life Go

The Buddha taught that suffering, dukkha, does not come simply from life itself, but from clinging.

In the **Dhammacakkappavattana Sutta (SN 56.11)**, he explained that the cause of suffering is craving (tanhā), the desire for things to be a certain way, the urge to hold on, and the tendency to resist what is unpleasant. This means that it is not life itself that creates dukkha, but the way we cling to it.

Letting go, then, does not mean letting go of life. It does not mean giving up people, responsibilities, or the things that matter. It means letting go of control, attachment, and craving, the constant need for things to be a certain way, and learning to accept life as it is.

By now, you may have begun to see that much of the struggle in the mind comes from trying to control what is happening. The mind wants to manage thoughts, remove discomfort, and secure certainty. It believes that if everything can be controlled, then peace will follow.

But the opposite happens.

The more you try to control thoughts, the more they return.

The more you try to eliminate anxiety, the stronger it feels. The more you try to force certainty, the more doubt appears. This is not because you are doing something wrong. It is because control itself creates tension.

This can be seen in simple ways in daily life. The more you try to fall asleep, the harder it becomes. The more you try to force your mind to be quiet, the louder it feels. The more you try to control a conversation or how someone sees you, the more tension you feel inside.

Control seems like the solution, but it often creates the problem.

The mind that is searching for a solution is often the same mind that created the problem.

In Buddhist wisdom, this is understood through the idea of craving, or tanhā, the desire for things to be different from how they are. We want pleasant experiences to stay, and we want uncomfortable ones to disappear. We want clarity instead of uncertainty, and control instead of allowing.

As taught in the **Dhammapada**, "From craving arises sorrow, from craving arises fear. For one who is free from craving, there is no sorrow, how then fear?" **(Dhammapada 216)**. This shows that the more the mind clings, the more it suffers.

Letting go is not about losing anything real. It is about releasing this inner struggle.

It is about letting go of control. Not every thought needs to be managed. Not every feeling needs to be removed. Not every situation needs to be resolved immediately. When you stop trying to control everything, the mind begins to soften.

It is also about letting go of attachment. Attachment is not about having things, it is about clinging to them as if they must stay the same. You can care for people without trying to control them. You can value your work without making it your identity. You can enjoy moments of happiness without fearing their loss.

In this sense, letting go is not losing anything meaningful. It is letting go of what was never truly yours to control in the first place.

It is like holding a handful of sand. If you hold it gently, it stays. But the tighter you grip, the more it slips through your fingers. In the same way, the more tightly you try to control thoughts, emotions, or life itself, the more unstable they feel.

Everything in life changes. People change. Situations change. Even your own thoughts and emotions change. Trying to hold everything in place creates tension, because life does not stay still.

When you begin to see this clearly, something shifts.

You stop holding on so tightly.

You begin to allow life to move.

This is where acceptance becomes important.

Acceptance does not mean you agree with everything or that you stop taking action where needed. It simply means you are no longer fighting reality. You see what is here, as it is, without adding resistance on top of it.

As the Buddha taught, "*Whatever is subject to arising is subject to cessation.*" Seeing this clearly, one begins to loosen the grip of clinging and move toward freedom from suffering.

In my own experience, this shift was gradual. At first, letting go felt uncomfortable. The mind would say, "You need to do something," or "You need to be sure." It felt like if I stopped controlling, things would fall apart.

But over time, I began to see something different.

The constant effort to control was what was creating the

pressure.

When I stopped trying to control every thought, they did not become stronger. They became quieter. Not immediately, but gradually. When I allowed emotions to be there without resisting them, they no longer felt overwhelming. They came, and they went.

There is a difference between practical action and mental control.

You can lock the door once, with awareness, and move on. You do not need to check it again and again to feel safe. You can prepare for something important, but you do not need to replay it endlessly in your mind. You can feel uncertainty, but you do not need to eliminate it completely.

This is where a sense of ease begins to return.

Not because everything is perfect, but because you are no longer fighting everything.

The mind begins to settle, not by force, but by release.

At first, the urge to control may still appear. This is natural. It is simply the old pattern continuing. But if you stay with awareness and do not react, the need to control begins to weaken.

And in that space, something changes.

There is less tension, less urgency, and less struggle.

You begin to see that you do not need to control everything to be okay.

Instead of trying to force life into a fixed shape, you begin to move with it.

Thoughts come and go. Emotions rise and fall. Situations change. But you are no longer trying to hold everything in place.

You are allowing things to be as they are.

And in that allowing, there is a quiet sense of freedom.

28

Awareness in Daily Life

Up to this point, you have begun to understand something important. Thoughts are not you. They have no fixed owner. Everything changes. There is no solid self behind your experiences. Much of suffering comes from clinging, reacting, and trying to control what cannot be controlled.

But understanding this is only the beginning.

The real shift happens when this awareness becomes part of your daily life.

Awareness is not something special or complicated. It is simply the ability to notice what is happening while it is happening. It is being present with your thoughts, your feelings, and your actions without immediately reacting to them.

Most of the time, the mind runs automatically. A thought appears, and you are already inside it. An emotion arises, and you are already reacting. A situation happens, and the mind immediately interprets it, judges it, or resists it. This all happens so quickly that it feels natural.

Awareness gently interrupts this pattern.

It creates a small space between what happens and how you respond. In that space, something new becomes possible.

You begin to see thoughts as they arise instead of being pulled into them. You notice emotions without immediately reacting. You become aware of your habits, your patterns, and your triggers.

This is not about stopping thoughts.

It is about seeing them clearly.

Awareness can be practiced in very simple ways. When you are walking, notice that you are walking. Feel the movement of your body and the contact of your feet with the ground. When you are eating, notice the taste, the texture, and the act of eating itself. These simple moments bring you back to what is actually happening.

When a thought arises, you can simply notice it: "This is a thought." When an emotion appears, you can notice it: "This is a feeling." Nothing more needs to be added. You are not trying to change anything. You are simply observing.

This is what is often referred to as mindfulness in Buddhist teaching, the practice of being aware of the present moment.

In the **Satipatthana Sutta**, the Buddha taught the foundations of mindfulness as observing the body, feelings, mind, and mental states clearly and directly, being "ardent, clearly knowing, and mindful, having put aside craving and distress with regard to the world." This is not a technique to control the mind. It is a way of understanding it.

The more you observe without reacting, the more you begin to see patterns. You notice how thoughts come and go. You notice how emotions rise and fall. You begin to see how reactions happen automatically when there is no awareness.

And slowly, something changes.

You are no longer completely identified with every thought. You are no longer reacting to everything immediately. There is space, and in that space, there is choice.

In daily life, this can be very simple. When anxiety arises, instead of immediately trying to remove it, you notice it. You feel it in the body and allow it to be there without adding resistance. When a thought appears, instead of analysing it, you observe it. When the urge to check, fix, or control appears, you notice the urge itself.

This is where everything begins to shift.

Because awareness weakens the cycle. You are no longer feeding every thought, every fear, or every habit. You are seeing them, and what is seen clearly begins to lose its power.

In my own experience, this was where things started to become real. Understanding helped, but awareness changed the way I lived. I began to notice thoughts instead of being trapped in them. I began to feel emotions without reacting immediately.

Slowly, the mind became quieter, not because life changed, but because my relationship with it changed.

Awareness does not remove challenges. It changes how you meet them. You still experience thoughts, emotions, and situations, but you are no longer completely controlled by them.

You are present.

And in that presence, there is a different way of living, one that is lighter, clearer, and less driven by fear or habit.

Awareness is not something you do once. It is something you return to again and again, in simple moments throughout your day.

And over time, this simple practice begins to transform

everything.

Over time, you begin to see something clearly.

The prison was never outside.

It was not in your circumstances, your past, or your thoughts themselves. It was in the way the mind reacted, clung, and became entangled in everything it experienced.

An invisible prison, built slowly through habit, fear, and misunderstanding.

For a long time, it feels real. Solid. Unbreakable.

But the moment you begin to observe your mind instead of fighting it, something begins to change.

The walls are no longer as strong.

Because what is seen clearly cannot control you in the same way.

You begin to notice thoughts without being trapped in them. You begin to feel emotions without being overwhelmed by them. You begin to see patterns instead of becoming them.

And slowly, something loosens.

Not because you forced it…

but because you finally saw it.

The prison was never made of real walls.

It was made of unconscious reactions, repeated patterns, and the belief that every thought needed to be followed.

And awareness begins to dissolve all of that.

Not by fighting…

but by seeing.

This is how the invisible prison begins to break.

29

Meditation: Awareness in Stillness and Movement

Meditation is often misunderstood. Many people think it means sitting still, stopping thoughts, or achieving a peaceful state. But in its true sense, meditation is not about forcing the mind to be quiet.

It is about observing the mind as it is.

Meditation is not the absence of thoughts or emotions. It is the presence of awareness, even when thoughts and emotions are there.

You do not need a special place or a fixed position. You can sit quietly, close your eyes, and simply notice what is happening. Thoughts will come. Feelings will arise. The mind may wander.

That is not a problem.

When you first try this, it may feel difficult. The mind may become louder. Thoughts may seem stronger. You may feel like you are not doing it right. This is natural. It does not mean meditation is failing, it means you are beginning to see the mind more clearly.

Instead of trying to control it, you simply observe.

You notice a thought: "This is a thought."

You notice a feeling: "This is a feeling."

And you allow it to be.

In this way, meditation is not separate from life. It is the same awareness you practice throughout the day, but in a quieter setting.

Over time, this simple observation strengthens your ability to remain present. It helps you see thoughts more clearly and react less automatically.

For someone dealing with overthinking or OCD, this can feel unfamiliar at first. The mind wants to analyse, fix, or control. Meditation shows a different way, not by solving every thought, but by learning not to follow every thought.

But meditation is not about perfection.

Even a few moments of awareness are enough.

There are also simple ways to practice this more intentionally. One is sitting meditation. You sit quietly and bring your attention to the breath. You notice the natural movement of breathing, without trying to control it. When the mind wanders, which it will, you gently notice it and bring your attention back to the breath. Not with force, but with patience.

Another is walking meditation. As you walk, you become aware of each step, the movement of your body, the contact of your feet with the ground, the rhythm of walking. Instead of being lost in thought, you are present with the movement itself.

These are not different practices. They are simply different ways of developing the same awareness.

In Buddhist teaching, this is part of right mindfulness, being aware of the body, the breath, the mind, and mental patterns as they arise. Not to control them, but to understand them.

In the **Satipatthana Sutta**, the Buddha encouraged observing the body, feelings, mind, and mental states clearly, with awareness and without clinging.

This is the heart of meditation.

Not controlling the mind…

but learning to see it clearly.

And the more clearly you see it,

the less power it has over you.

A Simple Way to Practice (Daily Life)

You do not need long sessions or perfect conditions to practice awareness.

You can begin in simple moments, exactly where you are.

Start with a few minutes. Sit quietly, or even remain where you are. Bring your attention to the breath. Not to control it, but to notice it. The natural rise and fall. The feeling of air moving in and out.

Thoughts will come. This is natural.

When they do, simply notice: "This is a thought."

And gently return to the breath.

You do not need to follow the thought.

You do not need to answer it.

Just return.

If a feeling arises, restlessness, anxiety, or discomfort, notice it in the same way: "This is a feeling." Let it be there without trying to change it.

Even a few moments like this are enough.

Throughout the day, you can bring this same awareness into ordinary activities. While walking, notice your steps. While eating, notice the taste and movement. While speaking, notice your words and reactions.

These are not separate from meditation.

This is meditation in daily life.

At times, you may forget. You may get caught in thoughts again. That is part of the process.

The practice is simply to notice, and return.

Not perfectly, but gently.

Over time, this small shift begins to grow. The space between thought and reaction becomes clearer. The urge to engage with every thought begins to weaken.

And in that space, something new becomes possible.

A quieter mind.

A lighter way of being.

A life that is no longer controlled by every thought.

30

Living This When Life Gets Difficult

Understanding the mind is one thing. Living this when life becomes difficult is something else.

It is easy to be aware when things are calm. When the mind is quiet, the body is relaxed, and nothing feels threatening, awareness comes naturally. But life does not always stay that way.

There will be moments of stress, fear, confusion, and emotional pain. There will be situations that trigger old patterns. There will be days when the mind feels heavy again, and thoughts begin to repeat.

This is where the real practice begins, not in perfect conditions, but in the middle of difficulty.

When something challenging happens, the mind reacts quickly. A thought appears, and it feels real. An emotion arises, and it feels overwhelming. The urge to fix, escape, or control becomes strong. In those moments, it may feel like everything you have learned disappears.

But it has not disappeared.

This is simply the mind returning to its old patterns, and

this is your opportunity, not to fight it, but to see it.

When anxiety arises, instead of immediately trying to remove it, pause and notice what is happening. Feel it in the body and let it be there without adding resistance. When thoughts begin to race, instead of analysing each one, step back and observe. You do not need to follow every thought. When the urge to check, control, or seek certainty appears, notice the urge itself and see it for what it is, the mind trying to feel safe.

That simple awareness begins to change your relationship with it.

This does not mean the feeling will disappear immediately. Sometimes it will stay for a while. Sometimes it will feel strong. But the difference is that you are no longer completely inside it. You are aware of it, and that awareness creates space.

In that space, the second arrow does not need to follow. The mind may still produce the first arrow, pain, discomfort, fear, but the second arrow, the reaction, the resistance, the story, does not have to take over. This is where suffering begins to reduce.

Not because life becomes easy, but because you are no longer adding extra layers to it.

Life will still bring difficulty. As the Buddha taught in the **Dhammacakkappavattana** Sutta, there is dukkha, discomfort, unease, and suffering, as part of human experience. This is part of being human. But suffering deepens when we resist it, cling to it, or try to make it something else.

The past is already gone, and the future has not yet arrived. What is real is this moment. When the mind keeps returning to what has happened or worrying about what might happen, it creates more struggle. But when you come back to what is here now, something begins to settle.

A common teaching in Buddhist wisdom is this: do not dwell in the past, do not become lost in the future, but return to the present moment. This points to a simple truth, clarity is always found in the present, not in mental replay or imagined outcomes.

There may still be difficult moments. There may still be days when the mind feels restless or unsettled. That is part of being human. The goal is not to remove all difficulty, but to meet it differently.

Instead of reacting with fear, you respond with awareness. Instead of trying to control everything, you allow things to unfold. Instead of believing every thought, you observe it.

In my own experience, this was not a straight path. There were times when I fell back into old patterns, when thoughts pulled me in, and when emotions felt overwhelming again. But something had changed.

Even in those moments, there was a small awareness in the background, a quiet knowing that this is happening in the mind. And that was enough.

Because each time you notice, even briefly, you weaken the pattern. Each moment of awareness is a step out of the cycle.

The Buddha also reminded that "*Whatever is subject to arising is subject to cessation.*" This means that even the most intense thoughts and emotions are not permanent. When you stop holding onto them, they begin to pass on their own.

You do not need to be perfect. You do not need to get it right every time. Even noticing after the reaction has happened is still awareness, and that still matters.

Over time, this becomes more natural. You begin to catch patterns earlier. You begin to react less automatically. You begin to trust that you do not need to control everything to be okay.

And slowly, something shifts.

Life still happens. Challenges still come. But you are no longer trapped in the same way.

The invisible prison may still try to appear, but it no longer holds you like it once did, because now you can see it.

And what is seen clearly cannot control you in the same way again.

31

Reflection: The Journey Back to Yourself

When I look back now, I can see that nothing outside of me truly changed. Life still brings uncertainty. Thoughts still arise. Emotions still come and go. Challenges still appear in different forms. But something inside changed. The way I see the mind is no longer the same.

For a long time, I believed that freedom meant getting rid of thoughts, fixing every feeling, and becoming a better, stronger version of myself. I believed that peace was something I had to reach somewhere in the future, after I had solved everything. But that was part of the prison, the constant trying, the constant fixing, the constant searching.

What I slowly began to see was much simpler. The problem was never the thoughts themselves. It was the way I related to them, the way I believed them, followed them, and tried to control them. When that began to change, everything began to shift. Not all at once, but gradually.

Before I came across Buddhist wisdom and practices, and met a monk who guided me, I had already explored different religions, paths, and teachings, hoping each one would finally give me the peace I was searching for. For a time, they seemed to help, but the confusion always returned. No matter what I followed, the struggle in the mind remained. The thoughts, the fear, the overthinking, they did not disappear. That is when I began to realise something important. It was not about finding the right label, belief, or system.

I did not convert to Buddhism, nor did I become a Buddhist. What I found was not a new identity, but a deeper understanding of my own mind, my thoughts, my suffering, and the way out of it. When I first met the monk, his words were simple: "**Be present. Be here now. Discover yourself**." At the time, I did not fully understand them. But over time, they became clear through direct experience.

At the same time, I want to say this clearly. I have deep respect for all religions, beliefs, and paths. Each one carries meaning, guidance, and value for those who follow it. This journey is not about criticising any path or saying one is better than another. It is simply about what I discovered through my own experience.

A key insight I gained through Buddhist wisdom and my own direct experience was this. As I continued to learn and reflect, I began to see something more clearly. Many of the conflicts, debates, and judgments I had witnessed in different religious settings were not necessarily caused by the religions or their teachings themselves, but by how people related to them.

Just as the root of overthinking is not the thought, but the reaction, the fear, and the need to control, I began to see a similar pattern here. The need to be right, to defend a belief, or to hold onto an identity can easily give rise to ego and division within faith communities. It often shows up in subtle ways. "My faith is the only true one." "My God is the only true God." "This is the only correct name." "This is the only way to be accepted." When these ideas are held tightly, they can create separation rather than understanding.

When I looked more deeply, I began to see what might be behind all this. It was not something outside of us, but something within. The same movement of the mind that seeks certainty, identity, and control. The same fear of being wrong, the same need to feel secure, and the same habit of holding on tightly.

Once I saw this clearly, it changed how I viewed other religions and faiths, not with judgment, but with a deeper sense of respect and understanding.

Because of this, I no longer feel the need to defend myself, my beliefs, or my understanding, nor to challenge or defend others. In this, there is a quiet sense of peace, one that I had not experienced before in the same way. It is not based on being right, but on understanding, on letting go, and on no longer being in conflict.

This naturally led me inward.

I understand that some may agree and others may disagree, and that is completely natural. The way I have understood Buddhist wisdom, practices, and teachings may be different from others, and that is okay. There is nothing here to defend or argue about. What I have shared comes from my own understanding and personal experience, what I have seen, lived, and learned for myself.

And perhaps that is all any of us can truly do, see clearly for ourselves, and allow others the space to do the same. This journey was never about being right. It was about seeing clearly, and finding peace within that clarity.

The real shift began when I turned inward and started to understand the mind itself. Through Buddhist wisdom, I came to see things differently, not as a system to follow, but as a way to observe and understand experience. It taught me to be mindful, to be present, and to live with greater awareness and compassion, towards others and towards myself. It also showed me the importance of harmlessness, not just in actions, but in the way I relate to my own thoughts and emotions.

For a long time, I felt like I had to keep striving, fixing, and becoming something better in order to find peace. There was always a sense that something needed to change, that I had to reach somewhere else to finally feel free. But through this understanding, something softened. Instead of constantly trying to become something else, I began to allow what is. I began to see that peace was not something to chase, but something that becomes visible when the struggle begins to settle.

There were still difficult days. There were still moments of fear, doubt, and confusion. But they no longer defined me in the same way. They became something I could observe rather than something I had to fight.

This is what changed everything. Not control. Not perfection. But awareness.

Awareness allowed me to step back from the noise of the mind. It allowed me to see thoughts as thoughts, feelings as feelings, and patterns as patterns. It allowed me to stop taking everything so personally. And in that space, something opened, a sense of ease, a sense of quiet. Not because life became perfect, but because I was no longer in constant conflict with it.

As the Buddha taught in the **Dhammapada,** *"All conditioned* *things are impermanent. When one sees this with wisdom, one turns away from suffering."* This is not just a teaching to understand, but something to see directly in your own experience.

Everything changes. Thoughts change. Emotions change. Even the patterns that once felt permanent begin to loosen when they are seen clearly. And with that, the grip of the mind begins to soften.

If you have come this far, you may have already started to see this for yourself, even in small moments, a pause before reacting, a thought noticed instead of followed, an emotion felt without resistance. These moments matter. They are not small. They are the beginning of freedom.

You do not need to become someone else. You do not need to fix everything. You do not need to reach a perfect state. You only need to see clearly, again and again, in simple moments, in ordinary life. This is the path, not a path of becoming, but a path of seeing.

The invisible prison was never made of real walls. It was made of misunderstanding, habit, fear, and the constant movement of the mind. And just as it was built slowly, it begins to dissolve slowly, through awareness, through patience, through seeing.

There may still be moments when the mind pulls you back. Moments when old patterns return. That is part of the journey. But now something is different. You can see it. And once you see it clearly, it cannot hold you in the same way again.

You may not feel completely free every moment. But you are no longer lost in the same way. And that matters.

Because freedom is not a final destination. It is something that begins the moment you start to see clearly, and continues each time you return to awareness.

This is the journey back, not to a new version of yourself, but to what has always been here. A quiet awareness. A steady presence. Freedom that was never outside of you, only waiting to be seen.

32

The Beginning of Freedom

Before you close this book, I want to thank you.

Thank you for giving your time, your attention, and your openness. This was not just a book to read. It was an invitation to look within. And by reaching this point, you have already taken that step.

Everything in this journey points to one simple truth.

The problem was never the thoughts.

The problem was our relationship with them.

The mind thinks. That is what it does.

Thoughts arise. Emotions come and go.

Nothing stays.

When we stop fighting, stop chasing, and stop identifying with every thought, something begins to shift. Not because we forced it, but because we finally allowed things to be as they are.

Peace is not something you create.

It is something you uncover when the noise is no longer believed.

You don't need to control the mind.

You don't need to eliminate thoughts.

You only need to see clearly.

And in that clarity, there is space.

In that space, there is freedom.

A Simple Way to See This for Yourself

Before you close this book, try this.

Sit comfortably.

Close your eyes.

Now do nothing.

Just wait.

Wait for the next thought to appear.

Don't try to think.

Don't force anything.

Just wait.

Soon, a thought will arise on its own.

Notice it.

Now ask yourself, did I choose that thought, or did it simply appear?

Stay with that for a moment.

Now try this.

Create a thought on purpose.

Say a word in your mind.

Notice the difference.

The first thought came on its own.

You did not choose it.

The second thought needed effort.

You had to create it.

Feel that difference.

One happens by itself.

The other is made.

The first thought is like a cloud drifting in the sky.
It appears on its own.
The second is like trying to draw a cloud with your hand.
It takes effort. You have to make it happen.
See what this shows.
Some thoughts happen to you.
They are not created by you.
And if they can arise on their own,
they can also pass on their own.
If a thought can appear on its own, then it is not fully you.
And if it is not fully you, you don't have to believe it, follow it, or fight it.
You can simply notice it and let it pass.
Thoughts come.
Thoughts go.
You remain the one who sees them.
Nothing you were looking for was ever outside.
Not peace.
Not clarity.
Not freedom.
It was always here, in the simple act of seeing.
Seeing a thought as a thought.
Seeing without holding.
Seeing without becoming.
And in that seeing, something begins to loosen.
And in that loosening, there is space.
And in that space, there is freedom.
Even if this feels subtle, stay with it.
This simple seeing is the beginning of freedom.
Insight is the beginning.
Practice makes it real.

The invisible prison was never locked.
It only needed to be seen.
And once it was seen clearly,
you were always free to walk out.

About the Author

Narinder Singh Chohan, known to many as Ricky, is an independent thinker with a deep interest in understanding the human mind, suffering, and inner transformation.

Born in India, he now lives in Australia with his wonderful wife and two amazing boys. He has spent years exploring different spiritual paths, religious teachings, and philosophical traditions in search of clarity and peace.

Through his personal journey with overthinking and OCD, he came to realise that true change does not come from external systems, but from understanding the nature of the mind itself. Drawing from lived experience and insights inspired by Buddhist wisdom, he focuses on helping others see their thoughts more clearly and relate to them in a healthier way.

In his spare time, he enjoys playing cricket with his boys.

In ***The Invisible Prison***, Narinder shares this journey with honesty and simplicity, offering readers a path towards greater awareness, inner peace, and freedom from mental struggle.

Made in the USA
Monee, IL
06 November 2026

67981963R00132